Voices 3

Canadians
Who Made a
Difference

Editor: Gladys E. Neale

P A A C
Foundation   "Together we will build a better future."

The addition of this resource to the
John M. Cuelenaere Public Library
was made possible by the Prince Albert &
Area Community Foundation
2008 Literacy Grant.

LLC

EACH ONE TEACH ONE

LAUBACH LITERACY OF CANADA

Voices 3: Canadians Who Made a Difference
Copyright © 1993 by Laubach Literacy of Canada
ISBN   0-920877-15-X   .

Canadian Cataloguing in Publication Data

Main entry under title:

Voices 3: Canadians who made a difference

ISBN 0-920877-15-X

1. Readers for new literates. 2. Readers — Canada —
Biography. 3. Canada — Biography. I. Neale,
Gladys E. II. Laubach Literacy of Canada.

PE 1126.N43V66 1993   428.6'2   C93-094748-7

Edited and typeset by Marsh Hill Publishing Services.

Printed and bound in Canada by D. W. Friesen, Altona, Manitoba.

Published by
Laubach Literacy of Canada,
P.O.Box 6548,
Station "A",
Saint John, New Brunswick,
E2L 4R9.

Contents

Introduction

This book of biographies of 20th Century Canadians has two purposes: (1) to give those who have just learned to read, or who have improved their reading skills, interesting stories at an easy reading level; (2) to make available to them biographies of Canadians who have made or are making a difference to Canadian culture, politics and business.

It is our hope, too, that these men and women will be role models for our adult students. Most of them achieved success through their own efforts and hard work.

Our sincere appreciation to the National Literacy Secretariat and the Department of Human Resources and Labour, whose generous grants enabled us to publish this book.

Laubach Literacy of Canada

Pilot Officer
Andrew C. Mynarski, V.C.

by

Michael Collins

The Victoria Cross is shown in this photograph of Andrew
Mynarski.

The Victoria Cross is given for bravery. It is the highest honour that can be awarded to a soldier, sailor, or airman. A young Canadian airman, Andrew Mynarski, won the Victoria Cross. He won it because he tried to save a trapped crewman. Their bomber was on fire and going down.

EARLY YEARS IN WINNIPEG

Andy was born in Winnipeg on October 16, 1914. He was the second son of Polish immigrants. His father died when Andy was sixteen. The Great Depression of the 1930s had begun. There was very little money. Andy left school and found a job. The extra money helped his mother to look after the Mynarski family.

WORLD WAR TWO

World War Two started in 1939. It spread quickly over most of the world. Thousands of young men were needed to fight in this war. Andy joined a Reserve Army regiment in Winnipeg. They trained on evenings and on week-ends. This meant he could still work at his job and help his family.

AN AIR WAR

At first there was very little action for soldiers in the war. But the navy and the air force were fighting. Aircrew were needed in large numbers. They trained aircrews in Canada. Men came from all over the world to train.

RCAF TRAINEE

Life was better now for the Mynarski family. Andy joined the Royal Canadian Air Force in September 1941 at Winnipeg. A week later he was sent to Manning Depot at Edmonton, Alberta. He was kept busy at the Depot. He was given his air force uniforms. There were lectures he had to attend. With other young men he drilled daily on the parade square. Doctors made sure he was healthy. There was little time to relax.

Andy was selected to train as a wireless operator/air gunner. He began his training at the Wireless Training School in Calgary, Alberta.

Andy in training.

TRAINING AS A
WIRELESS OPERATOR/AIR GUNNER

A wireless operator/air gunner on a bomber had two jobs. He handled all the messages of his crew to their base. He also sent wireless messages between his aircraft and other aircraft. His second job was to man a machine gun on a bomber.

Wireless messages were sent by Morse code during this war. This code is a series of long and short sounds. Some people find it hard to understand Morse code. Andy found he was one of those persons.

He was taken off the wireless operator/air gunner's course. He went to a Bombing and Gunnery School in Manitoba to train as an air gunner.

BRIEF TRAINING COURSE.

The air gunner's course lasted only a few weeks. Andy worked hard. He learned how to handle all his equipment as a gunner. He learned to identify all aircraft, friendly and enemy. Hours were spent flying in a gunnery aircraft. This taught him how to handle a gun turret. He learned how to fire machine guns at aerial targets that were towed by other aircraft. At last he finished the course.

He received his air gunner's wing just before Christmas. He was posted overseas. Andy had a short holiday with his family. On New Year's Day he was in Halifax. Then he sailed across the Atlantic Ocean to England.

OPERATIONAL TRAINING

In England Andy reported to a Personnel Reception Depot. He remained there for several weeks. In March 1942 he was sent to an Operational Training Unit. At this unit he flew in two types of bombers. He was taking advanced gunnery training. The training was done in the twin-engined Wellington bomber. The second bomber used for training was the larger four-motor Halifax. Andy's first flight over enemy territory was in a Halifax.

Halifax bomber in the air.

AIR GUNNER IN A LANCASTER BOMBER

Andy's bomber was part of a squadron of six aircraft. They were called the Moose Squadron. They had the picture of a moose painted on the side of their aircraft. Andy flew in Halifax bombers for a short time. Then his squadron changed to Lancaster bombers. The Lancasters were larger and faster than the Halifax bombers.

Andy was now a Flight Sergeant. He was part of the seven-man crew of the Lancaster. He was the mid-upper turret gunner. His gun turret was at the top of the Lancaster. Andy got along well with all the crew members. They liked the easy-going Andy. His particular friend was Flying Officer Pat Brophy, the Lancaster's rear gunner. These two airmen had the job of fighting off rear attacks on their bomber. Andy also kept the crew informed of the direction of these enemy attacks. The pilot of the Lancaster could then take action to save the bomber from attack.

Their bombing missions over enemy territory were successful. The crew and their aircraft always returned safely.

ANDY PROMOTED AGAIN

Andy was promoted to the rank of Warrant Officer. At that time the Allied Forces invaded Europe. The soldiers landed along the Normandy coast of France. The date of the invasion was June 6, 1944.

The troops needed a lot of air support. Bombing raids were made on enemy roads, bridges, and railroads. The raids helped to stop the enemy.

THE NIGHT RAID ON CAMBRAI

On the night of June 12, 1944 Andy's squadron was part of a bombing attack on Cambrai in France. Their target was the railroad yards. On the bombing run, Andy's aircraft was attacked by enemy aircraft. Andy's and Pat Brophy's machine guns kept the enemy fighters off. But Lancasters had a blind spot. It was directly under the bomber. In such an attack the machine guns of Andy and Pat could not point down at the enemy aircraft.

One of the enemy fighters managed to fly up under their Lancaster. The fighter opened fire with cannons. Shells ripped through the body of the Lancaster. The bomber caught on fire. Other cannon shells swept across the port wing of the bomber. The two port motors were ripped apart by the shells. The fuel tanks in the same wing burst into flames. The fire in the body of the bomber became more fierce. The flames were between Andy's turret and the rear turret.

BAILING OUT

The pilot of the burning Lancaster ordered his crew to bail out. The bomb-loaded Lancaster could blow up at any second. When the pilot bailed out he thought his crew had already escaped. But Andy was still in the bomber. It was not easy to get out of the mid-upper turret. When he reached the escape door in the side of the bomber he looked back. Flames were shooting higher inside the bomber. Through the flames he saw Pat Brophy trapped in his turret. Brophy was trying to get out but his turret was jammed.

Lancaster bomber.

ANDY TRIES TO SAVE
PAT BROPHY

Their aircraft was dropping lower. Andy was weighed down with his flying gear and parachute. He had to help Brophy escape and he had to do it quickly. There was not much room to move in the rear part of the bomber. Andy crouched then crawled back through the flames. The burning fluid smeared his flying suit. As he crawled along he pulled a fire axe from the side of the bomber.

He reached the rear turret. He shouted at his friend that he would free him. Brophy could not hear because of the noise. In the bomber's confined space Andy hacked at the jammed turret. The fire inside the aircraft spread and grew. Andy could not budge the turret. Brophy yelled and gestured at him to get out. He saw fire on Andy's flying suit. Andy knew what he meant. He tried to free the turret again but it would not budge. He nodded his head sadly to Pat's commands. Andy backed away through the fire. His flying suit soaked up more of the burning fluid. His parachute began to burn. He struggled to his feet at the escape door. He beat at his burning clothes with his gloved hands. But the efforts were useless. He looked back towards the trapped rear gunner. Andy stood up and saluted Pat Brophy. Andy was leaving his friend to die. Then Andy jumped.

French Resistance Fighters saw the flaming airman fall away from the bomber. Andy's parachute opened. It held together long enough to get him down. He landed in a swampy field. The French reached him as fast as they could.

THE BOMBER CRASHES

The burning bomber crashed some distance from where Andy had landed. It glided down and slid along the ground. Pat Brophy was still trapped in the turret. The port wing of the Lancaster hit a tree. The wing with the burning gas tanks ripped away. The bomber slid on, breaking up as it went. The rear turret was thrown to one side. Pat Brophy wasted no time getting out of the turret. He got away from the bomber and its load of bombs. He had escaped the crash with hardly any injuries. German soldiers found Brophy. He was sent to a German prisoner-of-war camp where he spent the remainder of the war.

All of the crew, except Andy, survived the crash. When the French Resistance Fighters reached Andy, they found him badly burned. He died before they could help him.

The crew of the bomber came to Winnipeg to honour Andrew Mynarski. Pat Brophy is the second to the left.

THE VICTORIA CROSS FOR
A BRAVE MAN

When the war ended Pat Brophy was freed as a war prisoner. He thought that Andy was still alive. When he found out what had happened, he told how Andy had struggled to save him. The story of Andy's unselfish bravery was impressive. It was recommended that he be given bravery's highest award. His mother received the Victoria Cross for her brave son.

Andrew Charles Mynarski had been promoted to Pilot Officer. He died without knowing about his promotion. He is buried at Meharcourt, France, with other airmen.

In the years after the war a housing project and a high school were named after Andy. Three small lakes in northern Manitoba were also named for him. They were thoughtful honours for the bravery of a young man. A young man who, long ago in the skies above France, tried to save a friend, a friend trapped in a burning bomber.

Here is a picture of the Andrew Mynarski ▶
Junior High School in Winnipeg.

ANDREW MYNARSKI SCHOOL

13

Chief Dan George
A Long and Active Life

by

Joan Maass

Dan receives the Order of Canada in full Native dress.

Chief Dan George lived many lives during his lifetime. He worked loading ships along the coast of British Columbia. He cut trees in the B.C. forests. He became a tribal chief. He went on the road as an entertainer. And, when he was almost seventy years of age, he achieved fame and fortune as a wonderful actor.

To start at the beginning, Chief Dan George was born in 1899. He was born on Burrard Indian Reserve No. 3, near Vancouver, British Columbia. His native name was Teswano. The missionaries who came later renamed him Dan George. Dan was the great-great-grandson of Chief Watsukl, head of the Tsla-a-wat Indian tribe. It was during Chief Watsukl's time that the Tsla-a-wats were forced to move from their inland home to the reserve where Dan was born.

A HAPPY CHILDHOOD

When Dan was a child it was his greatest joy to run and swim. He and his brother, with their cousins, would spend all day among the rocks and the waters of Burrard Inlet. His mother had a big orchard with hundreds of cherry and plum trees. Wild berries and fish were plentiful. He enjoyed a free and happy life before he was sent to school.

PAINFUL SCHOOL DAYS

When he was five years old Dan went to a missionary school in North Vancouver. The school was called St. Paul's. There he was forbidden to speak his own language, even at play. It was a frightening experience for a little boy. There were the nuns and priests in their long black robes. They spoke a strange language. He slept on a hard bed in a bare room. Everything was serious and grim. He was very lonely. He seemed to be punished all the time.

Every two weeks he was allowed to see his family. He would catch the streetcar. Then he would walk seven miles to get home on Friday night. On Sunday his Dad would drive him back by horse and buggy. Dan stood up to this hard life because he wanted to learn. But he had to leave the school at the age of sixteen. The government would not educate Native people past that age.

MARRIAGE

Dan went to work in the bush, making shingle bolts. He worked from sunup to sundown for two years. In 1918, when he was nineteen years old, he got married. His wife, Amy, was sixteen. She came from the Squamish tribe, who were neighbours of the Tsla-a-wats. Their marriage had been arranged by Dan's parents two years before. Dan bought a small old house from another Reserve. He moved it to his own Reserve and tried to fix it up. Their first child, Betty, was born. She died at the age of twelve. Betty was followed by Bob, their first son. There was also Rose, and little Glenna who died soon after she was born. And then came Ann and Irene and Marie and Lennie.

AMY

Amy was a wise and spirited woman. She wanted her children to remember the old ways of the Indian people. At the same time she tried to help them adapt to the new conditions being forced on them. Amy and Dan were married for fifty-two years. When Amy died in 1971, Dan and all the family missed her greatly.

Chief Dan with some of his grandchildren and great grandchildren. Amy is on his left.

WORK ON THE DOCKS

Dan began work as a longshoreman a year after his marriage. He got forty cents an hour. He worked at the vast port of Vancouver. He loaded lumber onto sailing ships. Sometimes men had to wait about the docks to be hired. Often they waited from seven in the morning until seven at night. Sometimes they stood in the freezing rain, only to be turned away without work. Work could go on for eighteen hours, many days without a food break. It was dangerous work, too. There were no safety nets below the high ladders from the docks to the decks of the big ships. Dan joined the longshoremen's union and helped fight for better conditions.

There were many strikes. Union members were beaten up by company police. The union was broken. Dan went back to work in the bush. He bought a team of horses and did logging on his own.

LIVING THROUGH THE DEPRESSION

Over the years 1930-1939 there was a world depression. During the "hungry thirties" Dan did anything he could. He dug clams and sold them for two cents a pound. He picked cascara bark and sold it to the drug companies for almost nothing. He picked berries and sold them in the city. He hunted and fished to feed his family. In 1936 Dan managed to get back on the waterfront. There he worked until 1947. At that time he was earning about a dollar and sixty cents an hour. After a serious accident he had to quit the waterfront. He went into construction work.

DAN HITS THE ROAD

In the early 1940's Dan began another adventure. He and his family started a travelling music group. They toured in a big blue wooden truck. The faded letters on the truck read: DAN GEORGE AND HIS INDIAN ENTERTAINERS. They would pack up the whole family and go hop picking. Then they would play three or four nights a week for dances in the little town halls. Rose, Irene, and Marie learned how to dance to Native songs. Bobby played the accordion. Dan played string bass. One of Dan's nephews played the mandolin. Later on Lennie played drums. They travelled hundreds of miles through British Columbia. Both Native people and white people came to their shows. For those days, they made a lot of money. People would give the girls $5.00 to sing a favourite song over again. They played western music—Hank Snow, Hank Williams—and cowboy tunes.

A LUCKY BREAK

Dan's first real break into "show biz" came in the early 1960s. At that time he was driving a city school bus. The Canadian Broadcasting Corporation was producing a TV series. It was called *Cariboo Country*. They were filming in the wild Chilcotin Valley in B.C. "Ol' Antoine" was an ancient Native man in the story. The white actor who played him fell ill and could not go on in the role. Dan's oldest son Bob had a small part in the show. The story is that he suggested that a real old Native might play the part. And so Dan's acting career began! He was superb in the role of Ol' Antoine. The series became an award-winner. Critics began to describe Chief Dan George as "one of the finest natural actors anywhere". He was following a deep instinct for theatre and magic gained from his Pacific Coast heritage.

Dan as "Ol' Antoine".

STARDOM IN THE THEATRE.

In 1967 Dan met the gifted playwright George Ryga. Ryga was working on his fine play *The Ecstasy of Rita Joe*. *Rita Joe* is the story of a Native girl who comes to the city to look for a better life. She is raped and murdered by the very people she hopes will help her. Th most deeply moving scenes in the play are those between Rita Joe and her father. Her father, played by Dan George, comes to the city to try to get Rita Joe to return to her village. When the play was produced at the Vancouver Playhouse, Dan's wonderful acting made him a star.

PHONE CALL FROM HOLLYWOOD

A movie was about to be made from one of the *Cariboo Country* TV stories in which Dan had starred. He was asked to come to Hollywood to try out for his role of Ol' Antoine. Dan was phoned from Hollywood. It was quite a shock. Amy urged him to go. She said it would be a favour for all the Native people. It would improve their image both to their own people and to non-Natives alike. In 1968, when Dan was 69 years old, he and Amy travelled to Hollywood. For his screen test Dan gave Chief Joseph's tragic speech of surrender to the white generals. Joseph was chief of the Nez Percé tribe of Idaho. His people were driven from their homes in 1873. Joseph's speech ended: "Joseph will fight no more forever!" Actors Glenn Ford and Keenan Wynn were in tears after Dan's speech. He made his screen test in one 15-minute take and landed the role.

THE HIT MOVIE: *LITTLE BIG MAN*

Dan's most famous movie role was "Old Lodgeskins" in *Little Big Man*. The story of *Little Big Man* included a massacre of Native people which took place in Oklahoma. General Custer and his United States Cavalry rode into a peaceful native village. They killed most of the people living there. Dustin Hoffman played "Little Big Man". The filming was a terrible time for everyone. It was done near Calgary in bone-chilling weather. The wind-chill factor sent the temperature down to -50 degrees Celsius. But Dan stood the cold better than the other much younger actors.

Dan relives the past by tracking and killing this 2000-pound buffalo in the Northwest Territories.

The release of *Little Big Man* brought rave reviews from the critics. It changed forever the Hollywood view of the Indian. It brought movie stardom to Chief Dan. He won the New York Film Critics' Award. He was nominated for an Academy Award. But Dan's joy was mixed with great sorrow. A few weeks later his wife Amy died.

Arriving home from New York to the greetings of friends and family.

MORE FILMS, AWARDS, AND
DINNER WITH THE QUEEN.

The years following the making of Little Big Man were very hectic. Dan worked on many films. He had a role with Bob Hope in *Cancel my Reservation*. He starred in *Alien Thunder*, with Donald Sutherland. When Queen Elizabeth visited B.C., Dan was guest of honour at a state dinner. The dinner was held aboard the royal yacht "Britannia". He was made an Honorary Doctor of Laws by Simon Fraser University. At the ceremony he found himself sitting opposite the former chairman of B.C. Hydro. B.C. Hydro stood for everything that Dan and his people detested. Due to this company's work, rivers had been dammed, land had been wasted, and wildlife destroyed.

Despite his fame and acclaim, Dan did not "go Hollywood". He often returned to his small home at Burrard Inlet. "I was born here. And I'm gonna die here," he said.

Chief Dan George died on September 12, 1981.

The funeral service for Chief Dan George was simple. ▶
1200 family and friends came to mourn his passing.
He was 82 years old.

25

Lucy Maud Montgomery

by

Freda Hudson

THE EARLY DAYS

Many people have seen the CBC program *Anne of Green Gables*. They have learned to love Anne. They know the names of Marilla and Matthew. They know about Avonlea. But how many know the name of the person who created Anne? Her name is Lucy Maud Montgomery. She was known to her family and friends as Maud.

Prince Edward Island was home to Lucy Maud Montgomery. She was born there on November 30, 1874. Her mother was a MacNeill. The MacNeills had been one of the first three families to settle in Cavendish. They had settled there in the late 1770s. They were very proud of their history.

Lucy Maud Montgomery was born in a small wooden house. The house was in the village of Clifton. Clifton is now called New London. Her mother was Clara NacNeill Montgomery. Her father was a local merchant. His name was Hugh John Montgomery. They named her Lucy after Clara's mother. They named her Maud after a daughter of Queen Victoria. Her mother, Clara, was one of six children. Hugh John had eight brothers and sisters. Lucy Maud had thirty-five first cousins. She was quite different from the orphan Anne of Green Gables. Anne did not have cousins. But in many other ways Anne and Maud were alike.

LOSS OF PARENTS

When she was four years old, her mother died. She died of T.B. (tuberculosis).

Her father had once worked as a sea captain. He was restless. Clara's mother and father had not approved of the marriage. Hugh was 13 years older than Clara. Maud loved her father. He was charming and popular. But he was not a good business man. After the death of his wife his storekeeping business failed. Clara and Maud had moved into the MacNeill home when Clara was sick. When she died, Maud's grandparents wanted to keep her. They would raise her. Her father did not object. When Maud was seven, her father went to Saskatchewan for the summer. He went there many times. Finally he stayed in Saskatchewan.

Farmhouse in Cavendish.

CAVENDISH

Maud continued to live with her grandparents. They lived in a farmhouse in Cavendish. Her grandparents were very strict. When Maud was very young she created two imaginary friends. One was Katie Maurice. The other was Lucy Gray. Her imaginary friends would keep her company. She was a lonely child.

When she was seven, her grandparents invited two orphans to live with them. They were Wellington and David Nelson. The boys lived there for three years. They were happy years for Maud. She had someone to play with. She had someone beside her imaginary friends. They built a playhouse near the orchard. They would frighten themselves by telling ghost stories. Long after the boys left, Maud was still afraid of evil spirits. Nothing frightened her more than the "Cavendish Road Woods".

CHILDHOOD

Maud's childhood was not easy. She had many fears. She also had a hot temper. It was easy to hurt her feelings. She wanted to be just like other children. Her grandparents did what they thought was best. In good weather, the other children went to school barefoot. But her grandparents made her wear boots. The other children took their lunch to school. Maud had to go home to a hot dinner at noon. Her stories about Anne were stories about Maud and Maud's early life. The grandparents lived by their rules. It was hard for Maud to understand.

Cavendish kitchen.

Maud's grandparents were not young when they adopted her. Maud and her grandmother were quite different. Her grandmother was cold and strict. Maud loved books. Her grandmother thought she read too much. Maud's friends were not welcome in the house. Maud was often reminded that she owed everything to the grandparents. Nothing to her father!

TRAVEL TO PRINCE ALBERT

In 1890 her father sent for her. Maud was now 15. She was sorry to leave her friends. She was happy to be leaving her grandparents. She left Prince Edward Island with her other grandfather, Senator Donald Montgomery. They went by ferry to the mainland and then by train to Saint John, New Brunswick. There they changed trains. Six days after leaving the Island they reached Regina. Her father met them there. She had not seen him for five years. The next day they went 200 miles north to Prince Albert.

LIFE WITH FATHER

Hugh John Montgomery had done well in Prince Albert. He had a good job and was a town councillor. He had a big house. He had married Mary Ann McRae. Mary and Hugh John had a two-year-old daughter, Kate. Maud had been writing to her stepmother for three years. She thought that she would be happy with her. This was not to be. Mary was cruel to Maud. She had a bad temper. She nagged Hugh John. She nagged Maud. She was jealous of her. In 1891 there was a second child born. Maud was treated like a servant. She was looking after both babies. She was doing most of the housework.

In a letter home, Maud wrote, "I hate Prince Albert more every day I stay in it." Even so, she had some good friends.

Eight months after Maud had arrived in Prince Albert, she wanted to go home. She was homesick. She was unhappy. In August 1891 she left. Her father was sorry to see her go. But he understood. Life with Mary was not easy.

FIRST PUBLICATIONS

All through the years Maud wrote. She kept a journal. She wrote poems and stories. She sent one of her poems to the Charlottetown paper. To her delight, they printed it!. This encouraged her. She entered an essay competition run by the Montreal "Witness". Her essay was published. Then the "Patriot" published it. The Prince Albert "Times" published her essay, "A Western Eden". Other newspapers copied it. At the age of 16, Maud's work appeared in newspapers in both eastern and western Canada.

HOME AGAIN

Maud was so happy to be home. When she arrived at her grandparents' home, she hugged them both. After life with Mary, her grandparents did not seem so bad. She visited the schoolhouse. She visited her old friends.

Her grandfather suggested that she write the story of her trip. She wrote a report on the trip from Prince Albert. She sent it to the newspaper the "Patriot". They were happy to print it. Maud had been writing for a long time. She still wondered if she would ever be a real author. She had a lot of dreams. She wanted to be an author. She wanted to go to college. She had no money of her own. Her grandparents thought that no girl needed more education. They thought high school was enough.

PARK CORNER

Early in 1892 Maud agreed to teach her cousins Clara, Stella, and George to play the organ. She spent four months with them at Park Corner.

The three girls had something more than music on their minds — boys! The girls were teenagers and pretty. The young men wanted to walk them home from meetings. They met at the Park Corner Literary Society. The young men also took them for drives by horse and buggy. "Dating" was not the same as today. Life was simple. There were not many things for young people to do.

Maud had a picture of her ideal lover in her mind. None of the young men that she knew could compare with the man of her dreams.

Maud as a student.

RETURN TO SCHOOL

She continued to write. Finally, her grandparents allowed her to return to school. She went back to the Cavendish school. There she studied for the entrance exams. The entrance exams were for the Prince of Wales College in Charlottetown. She hoped that she would earn her teacher's licence. She stayed at the school for a year.

When Maud went to Charlottetown to write the exams, she was very nervous. The English exam came first. She knew that she was good in English. After English came French and agriculture. All in one day she had to write Latin, algebra, and geometry. Then she worried for two weeks. But when the pass lists came, she was very happy. Out of 264 she had finished fifth! Maud was going to college!!

COLLEGE

Charlottetown was only twenty-four miles away. To Maud it seemed a long way. She hated leaving Cavendish and her friends.

In Charlottetown Maud lived five blocks from the College. She lived at a boardinghouse. Another one of her cousins joined her there. The boardinghouse was not very comfortable. The meals were not good. Maud was always hungry. The boardinghouse keeper was also stingy with coal. In the winter the house was always cold. One winter morning Maud woke to find two inches of ice in her water jug!

While she was in college she worked very hard. But all her hard work was worth it. Out of 120 students, only 49 passed. Maud had done the two-year program in just one year. She finished sixth out of the 49. Then she had to write the exam to become a teacher. She was in fifth place out of 18.

LOOKING FOR A JOB

Now she had to look for a job. Her grandfather was not much help. He thought a salesclerk's job would be good enough. He would not drive Maud to interviews at schools. He wouldn't even lend her a horse so that she could go by herself. She had to write for the jobs. Often her letters were not answered. Finally she got a job in Bideford. She taught there for a year.

HALIFAX

She still wanted to write. She wanted to be a writer. She was too poor to pay for the four-year program needed to get her degree. So she went to Dalhousie College in Halifax for a year. Not many women went to college in the 1890s. Dalhousie College graduated the first woman in its history in 1885. While she was in Halifax Maud won a writing contest. The contest was run by the Halifax "Evening Mail". She was paid $5.00. This was the first money she received for anything she wrote. She had been sending her work to newspapers and magazines for six years. Suddenly it was paying off. She continued to write and send her work to magazines. In one month she was paid $22.00 for two poems and one story. A young woman could do a lot with $22.00 in those days! She could buy a pair of boots for 95 cents. Lambskin gloves cost 49 cents. She could buy a book for 25 cents.

TEACHING

After her year in Halifax, she returned to the Island. She spent months trying to get a teaching job. She found one in Belmont, forty miles from Cavendish. It was in Belmont that men became more important in her life. She was now 22 years old.

Maud did not like Belmont. She called it "a wretched old hole". She lived at the house of Mr. and Mrs. Fraser. She was not happy there. Her room was like a jail cell. It was small, cold, and dark. To get away from the Frasers she would visit the Simpsons.

THE SIMPSONS

The three Simpson boys were Maud's second cousins. The boys all loved Maud. The third son, Edwin, was at college. He started to write to Maud. In his fourth letter he told her that he loved her. They hardly knew each other! She did not love him, but they shared the same interest in literature. When he came home from college for a holiday, he asked her to marry him. Maud said "yes". They agreed that the engagement would be kept a secret. Edwin would finish his education first. It was not long before Maud knew she had made a terrible mistake. She didn't know what to do. On Prince Edward Island in the 1890s, a marriage proposal was very serious.

HERMAN

In 1897-98 she was teaching in a village called Lower Bedeque. There she lived with a family named Leard. She liked them. She liked their children. The oldest was 27 years old. His name was Herman. He and Maud got along very well. They joked, laughed, and teased each other. One night, returning from a party, Herman kissed Maud. She fell madly in love with him! But Maud knew that they could never be happy together. They were seeing each other secretly. Each time they were together, she swore that it must end. She was still engaged to Edwin. At Christmas Edwin came to visit.

Maud was sick with love and longing. But she knew she had to end it. In the spring of 1898 she kissed Herman for the last time. Then she went home to Cavendish to care for her grandmother.

In 1900 her father died. He was only 59.

HOME AGAIN

She had to go home. Her grandfather MacNeill had died. Her grandparents had had five children. None of them wanted to take care of their mother. Maud felt that she had to do it. They had taken care of her. She thought that it was her duty. Maud would give up teaching. She would live in Cavendish with her grandmother. She would help her grandmother run the post office. The post office was in the farmhouse.

At first Maud was happy to be back home. She visited relatives. She went to the Literary Society meetings, concerts, and church teas. But her life with her grandmother was difficult. The old woman was very hard to live with. She was rude to visitors. So Maud would not invite anyone to the house. She was getting bored. She continued to write, and this helped her. She sold stories to American magazines.

THE NEWSPAPER

In 1901 her first cousin Prescott MacNeill agreed to live with his grandmother. This made it possible for Maud to move to Halifax. She worked for a newspaper. The newspaper was called "The Daily Echo". She was 27 years old. She enjoyed being the only woman working with the men at the newspaper. Everyone liked her.

She was working nine hours a day, but she kept on writing. During the nine months in Halifax she sold more than 30 stories. She went home for her holidays. The newspaper wanted her to return. But her cousin had made her grandmother unhappy all winter. So, doing her duty, Maud stayed with her grandmother.

Maud at the time she worked in Halifax.

Room in which Maud did most of her writing.

RETURN TO CAVENDISH

The next few years were often miserable. Her grandmother was becoming impossible. It was in those years that she wrote *Anne of Green Gables*

Maud dated some of the young men in Cavendish. But she never felt about them as she had about Herman. To fight against her loneliness, she wrote to pen-pals.

Maud knew that her future was dark. When her grandmother died she would have no home. John MacNeill would get the farm. Maud would be homeless. She would get no thanks for the work that she had done. She had looked after her grandmother. She had run the post office. She had suffered her grandmother's bad temper.

Ewan MacDonald.

EWAN MACDONALD

In 1903 a new minister came to her church. His name was Ewan MacDonald. He lived in a village nearby. So Maud only saw him at church. Two years later he moved to Cavendish. Maud saw him more often. He came to the post office to get his mail. The more he came, the more she liked him. They talked about many things. She began to look forward to his visits.

In 1906 he went to Scotland to study. Before he left he asked Maud to marry him.

She knew she would never love him the way she had loved Herman. But he offered a life of happiness. She would not be lonely anymore. She said "yes". But they would have to wait. They would wait until Maud was not needed at home.

In March 1911, Lucy MacNeill died. She was 86 years old. Four months later, Maud and Ewan were married. He had waited for five years. Maud was 36 years old. They went to Britain by ship for their honeymoon. The honeymoon lasted two months.

Lucy Maud — 61 years of age.

LEASKDALE, ONTARIO

When they returned to Canada they lived in Leaskdale. Leaskdale is a village just north of Toronto, Ontario. In 1912 her first son was born. He was called Chester Cameron MacDonald. Three years later her second son was born. They named him Ewan Stuart MacDonald. Maud was now forty years old. Every summer the family visited Prince Edward Island. She was a good wife and mother. She worked with the Sunday School, the Women's Missionary Society, the Young People's Guild, and the Ladies' Aid. She visited the sick. She went to weddings and funerals. But she still wrote for three hours every morning. She still had her black moods. She also had to cope with her husband's fits of severe depression. Her marriage was not her romantic dream. But she was loved and cared for. She could keep on writing.

The Manse at Leaskdale.

The parlour at the Manse.

L.M. MONTGOMERY
WORLD FAMOUS AUTHOR

Maud died in 1942 at the age of 68. She is buried in a cemetery near Lover's Lane in Cavendish. By then, she had written 22 novels. Her goal was to be a successful writer. When *Anne of Green Gables* was published, she proved that she was. Today *Anne* is published in Danish, Finnish, French, Hebrew, Icelandic, Italian, Japanese, Korean, Norwegian, Portuguese, Slovak, Spanish, and Turkish.

The television programs of Anne and other people in Maud's books have been shown all over the world.

L. M. Montgomery belongs not only to Canada but to the world!

Lincoln Alexander

by

Jan Sanderson

Lincoln Alexander was born in Toronto, Ontario on January 21, 1922. His father, also named Lincoln, was from Jamaica. Mae Rose, Lincoln's mother, was from an island called St. Vincent.

Lincoln's mother wanted her son to get an education. She believed if he did, he could get a job.

Lincoln went to school at Riverdale Collegiate in Toronto. He was the only black person in the school. The other children would call him names because he was black. This was a difficult time for Lincoln. He got into a lot of fights with the other boys.

NEW YORK

When Lincoln was fourteen years old, his parents' marriage ended. Lincoln and his mother moved to the United States. They lived in New York. He went to school there. The Alexanders lived on a street with other black people. Lincoln's friends on the street did not go to school.

His first job was at a bowling alley. The young Lincoln Alexander did not like being treated unfairly. At this job Lincoln started to speak up for the rights of black people. Many people did not want to hear what he had to say.

BACK TO CANADA

A few years later, Lincoln and his mother moved back to Canada. The Second World War had started in Europe. Lincoln's mother wanted him to help Canada in this war.

Lincoln waited to be called for service in the war. During this time he continued his high school studies. At night after school, Lincoln took a course in machinery. He did not know yet what he wanted to do with his life.

Lincoln met a girl named Yvonne. He moved to Hamilton, Ontario to be near her. He was in grade 13 when he was called into war service. Lincoln served in the Royal Canadian Air Force (RCAF). He was a wireless operator.

Lincoln learned a lot when he was in the Air Force. He learned to respect people in authority. Lincoln travelled a lot in Canada. He became very proud of his country. In the Air Force, Lincoln met people from all over the world. He was learning a lot about people.

IMPORTANCE OF EDUCATION

After the war, Lincoln went back to finish grade 13. He became friends with a classmate. His friend's name was John Miller. When Lincoln and John graduated from high school, they went to McMaster University in Hamilton.

Lincoln's family did not have much money. Luckily, the Air Force helped to pay for his education. Lincoln's grades had to be very good for him to get the money. Lincoln worked very hard at school. He graduated in 1949 with a Bachelor of Arts degree.

Today, when Lincoln Alexander looks back on his life, he realizes the importance of education. He says: "You've got to get your education. Life is tough enough as it is without education; with it, more doors are opened, life gets less tough."[1]

LAW SCHOOL AND MARRIAGE

Lincoln wanted to be a lawyer. He went to Osgoode Hall Law School in Toronto. His high school friend, John Miller, went to the same school.

Lincoln was in law school when he married Yvonne. They had one child. His name is Keith.

Lincoln and Yvonne.

TAKING A STAND

A few months before he graduated from law school, Lincoln Alexander's life changed.

In class one day, a professor said something bad about black people. Lincoln was normally a very quiet student. But on this day he could not keep quiet. He had to reply to the professor. Lincoln told the professor he was wrong to say nasty things about people. The professor was angry with Lincoln for speaking as he did.

After class, most of Lincoln's classmates were glad he had defended black people. They thought the professor was wrong to say bad things about people. They said Lincoln was right.

Lincoln Alexander was proud of himself for defending black people. He learned it was important to say what you think is right. Since that day, Lincoln Alexander has always defended people who have needed help.

Lincoln Alexander graduated from law school in 1953. He got a job as a lawyer. In 1962 Lincoln and his high school friend, John Miller, started a law firm. There were two other lawyers who worked with them. Lincoln Alexander was the first black lawyer in the City of Hamilton. This was the beginning of the many "firsts" in his life. He was a successful lawyer.

POLITICAL CAREER

Prime Minister Diefenbaker wanted Lincoln to enter politics. Lincoln had never thought of politics as a career. In the 1960s there were no black people in the government. For this reason, Lincoln decided to enter politics.

In 1965 Lincoln Alexander ran as a Conservative Party candidate. He ran against seven other people in the Hamilton West area. He lost the election.

In 1968 Lincoln tried again and was elected. His friend John Miller helped him to win the election.

Lincoln Alexander became the first black Member of Parliament. He was re-relected in 1972, 1974, 1979, and 1980. Lincoln Alexander was an Observer to the United Nations in 1976 and 1978.

In 1979 he was asked to be a cabinet minister. Lincoln became the first black cabinet minister. He was the Minister of Labour.

Labour Minister in the rain.

WORKERS' COMPENSATION BOARD

In 1980 Lincoln lost the election. Premier Bill Davis of Ontario asked Lincoln to take charge of the Workers' Compensation Board. He accepted the job. Lincoln was the first black person to have this job.

AN OFFER HE COULD NOT REFUSE

In 1985 Lincoln Alexander was asked by Her Majesty the Queen and the Prime Minister of Canada to be Ontario's next Lieutenant Governor. Lincoln was honoured and accepted the job. He was Canada's first black Lieutenant Governor.

THE DUTIES OF THE LIEUTENANT GOVERNOR

The Lieutenant Governor of Ontario represents the Queen in the province. The Lieutenant Governor has many duties. There are too many to mention all of them.

When members of the Royal Family, representatives from other countries, important Canadians and heads of state visit Ontario, they are welcomed by the Lieutenant Governor. Some of the people Lincoln met were Nelson Mandela, Ronald Reagan, and the Queen Mother.

The Lieutenant Governor attends religious, cultural, recreational, and educational events. His staff plans receptions, luncheons, and dinners for guests.

As Lieutenant Governor Lincoln Alexander gave the Throne Speech. The Throne Speech is given at the beginning of every new session of Parliament. This speech introduces the topics to be discussed at that session.

Lincoln Alexander reading the Throne Speech.

MORE DUTIES

On New Year's Day, the Lieutenant Governor has a reception at Queen's Park. Everyone is welcome to come to this affair.

The Lieutenant Governor's job has changed over the years. Now the Lieutenant Governor is more involved with community issues.

A BUSY MAN

With over ten million people in the province of Ontario, Lincoln Alexander was very busy. He worked 14-hour days, seven days a week. Lincoln loved his job. He wanted to help people.

During his time in office, Lincoln Alexander wanted to help young people. He told them about the importance of education. He encouraged young people to be the best they could be. He told them to stay away from alcohol and drugs.

Lincoln also wanted to improve the way people from different cultures and backgrounds got along together. He worked hard with different community groups.

Lincoln Alexander spent a lot of time visiting communities outside Toronto. He visited schools and attended many events all across Ontario.

Newspaper, television, and radio reporters liked Lincoln Alexander. They often referred to him as the "Linc" between the Queen and the province.

The position of Lieutenant Governor is usually for five years. A few months before the end of Lincoln Alexander's term, Prime Minister Brian Mulroney asked him to stay longer. Lincoln Alexander was the Lieutenant Governor of Ontario for over six years.

Here Lincoln talks with students in a school during history
week.

Lincoln, his family and first grandchild.

RETIREMENT

Lincoln Alexander retired as Lieutenant Governor on September 20, 1991. Many people were sad to see him go. Lincoln Alexander said this about his life as Lieutenant Governor.

"I'll miss this wonderful life.... I'll miss all the wonderful things that happened; I'll miss the people from all around Ontario... their kindness, their generosity, their warmth. But I'll miss the young people most; I've taken a great interest in the young people and, of course, won't have the same opportunities to counsel them."[2]

RECEIVED MANY AWARDS

Lincoln Alexander has received many awards. Some of the awards he received were The Man of the Year award from the Ethnic Press Council of Canada in 1982. By the House of Commons, he was awarded the Certificate of Service Award.

In 1985 Lincoln received an award in honour of his old friend, former Prime Minister John Diefenbaker. The award is called the Canadian Award John G. Diefenbaker Memorial Foundation.

Lincoln has received honorary degrees from a number of universities.

As an Osgoode Hall graduate between the years of 1889 and 1960, Lincoln was awarded a Doctor of Laws degree by York University.

He was awarded the Silver Acorn from the Boy Scouts of Canada. This award was presented to Lincoln Alexander by the Governor General of Canada.

In 1992 he received the Order of Canada. Lincoln Alexander was also awarded the Order of Ontario.

EARNED GREAT RESPECT

Lincoln Alexander has been involved with many community organizations. He has earned the great respect of many people. Former Mayor of Hamilton Bob Morrow said:

"(Lincoln's) own personal standards are very high and he has become an example to those around him and to those who observe him."[3]

THE MAN HIMSELF

In 1993 Lincoln Alexander turned 71 years old. He is spending more time gardening, reading, listening to music and playing with his grandchildren.

Lincoln's grandchildren make him want to live longer. He wants to see them grow and experience life. He is enjoying the extra time he has to spend with his wife and family.

Lincoln Alexander is a determined man. He is determined to make this country a better place to live for all people.

Lincoln admires people like Duke Ellington, a very talented and well-spoken musician. He admires Martin Luther King, one of the first people to speak up for the rights of black people.

Lincoln Alexander speaks very highly of his wife, Yvonne. He admits that without her support and strength, he could not have done what he did to help other people.

His only son, Keith, is an investment counsellor. He and his wife and two children live in Hamilton. Keith says his father taught him to respect people and to be honest with them.

"I like being around him," Keith said, "If I have a bad week, I spend half an hour with my parents and they have me laughing."[4]

Apart from getting married, one of the greatest moments of Lincoln Alexander's life was meeting Queen Elizabeth. Her Majesty knew about his family and his job. Lincoln said she was an intelligent and dignified woman. He was very impressed by her.

Lincoln Alexander is a kind and generous man. He always has a twinkle in his eyes and an easy smile. It is easy to understand why so many people like him. There is no doubt that Lincoln Alexander also likes people.

FOOTNOTES

[1] Susan Welstead, *The McMaster Times*, Winter 1992
[2] Royson James, *Toronto Star*, April 9, 1992
[3] Royson James, *Toronto Star*, April 9, 1992
[4] Barbara Turnbull, *Toronto Star*, October 29, 1989

Kick-off ceremonies at the Vanier Cup in 1987.

The Story of
Margaret Laurence

by

Bernice Cleator

"I BELIEVE ..."

"I believe we have to live, as long as we live, in the hope of changing the world for the better .... It is not too late ... with all our doubts, with all our flaws, and with all our problems, I believe that we will carry on, with God's help."[1]

These are the words of Margaret Laurence, one of the most important writers of our time.

Margaret Laurence died in 1987 at the age of 60. Through her writing, she left us her thoughts on what it is to be a woman and a human being. She dared to write of the joy and pain of conception, birth, and the raising of children. She wrote also of sadness at the loss of loved ones. She believed strongly in the importance of every human being. She believed in the need for freedom and justice for all. Many people were not ready for her kind of writing.

EARLY DAYS

In 1926 she was born Margaret Wemyss in a small town in Manitoba called Neepawa. Her father was a young lawyer and her mother was a pianist. Her mother's three sisters, Margaret's aunts, were close to the family. There were many happy times. When Margaret was four, her mother died. One of the aunts, a teacher of English literature in Calgary, came home to look after her. A year later this favourite aunt married her father and became her "Mum". That is what Margaret always called her. Margaret's brother Robert, called after their father, was born in 1933.

---

[1] This quotation and all the others in the story are from:
Laurence, Margaret: *Dance on the Earth*, a memoir.
McClelland and Stewart Inc., Toronto, 1989.

Mum, Margaret, and Dad.

ONLY THREE IN THE FAMILY

Margaret wrote with love of her first desk. It was restored and painted bright blue by her father for a Christmas gift. A month later her father died of 'flu. Margaret was nine. Now the family was down to three: Mum, Margaret, and baby brother Robert.

Margaret, aged six.

DOORS WERE OPENING

Some years before, Margaret's father had built her a play house with windows. It had boxes full of flowers. There in the back garden, it was Margaret's very own place. There she read all the books she could get her hands on. But she not only read. She filled five-cent notebooks with her own stories. Mum was always ready to listen and to encourage her.

In high school her chief joys were writing for the school newspaper and studying English literature. "I felt as though a whole series of doors were opening in my mind," she later wrote.

Margaret and her brother Bob.

THE WAR, 1939-1945

Then came the war. Young Margaret was filled with rage when she saw the boys of her town marching off to fight. They were not much older than herself. To the end of her life, Margaret hated violence of any kind: she hated violence between nations, between classes, between races, in families, against women.

MARRIAGE

At eighteen Margaret went to the University of Manitoba. There she won prizes in literature. She graduated in the spring of 1947. The same year, at 21, she met and married Jack Laurence. He was an engineering student at the university. Jack had spent the war years in the Air Force. He was ten years older than Margaret. The young couple took an apartment in Winnipeg. Margaret worked for a newspaper while Jack finished his degree in engineering.

ADVENTURES ABROAD

After his graduation, Jack took Margaret to England in 1949. There he began a career of building railways, bridges, seaports, and dams. His work took them to Somaliland, then on to Ghana, both in Africa. Their first child, a girl named Jocelyn, was born in England in 1952. The Ghana years were happy. Jack was building a seaport. They were young and in love, and they had a beautiful little girl. At the age of 28, Margaret had her second child, a boy, David. He was born in 1955.

"I saw my son at the moment of his birth, before the cord was severed, I felt as though I were looking over God's shoulder at the moment of the creation of life," she wrote in her memoirs.

MUM'S LAST ILLNESS AND
MARGARET'S FIRST NOVEL

Back at home, Margaret's Mum fell ill. Margaret left Ghana with her two young children. She flew halfway around the world to be with Mum for the last months of her life. During the years in Africa, Margaret had been writing her first novel, called *This Side of Jordan*. It was based on what she had seen of life in that country. She showed it to her Mum.

"It was as if the illness, for some hours, fell away. She analyzed my novel.... It was her final gift to me." The novel was published in 1960, three years after her Mum's death. It won an important award.

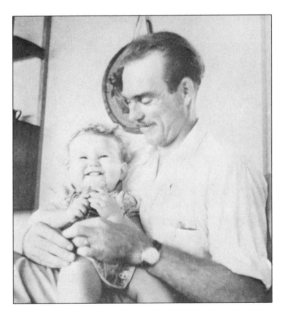

Jocelyn with her father.

VANCOUVER

After Jack returned from Ghana, the family lived for five years in Vancouver. Margaret was trying to do three jobs: being a wife, a mother, and a writer. "My sense of being torn apart, in those five years in Vancouver, was severe."

She wrote five books about Africa. Suddenly she felt herself called to write something very different. "An old woman had come into my mind. I suppose she had been there for a while, but all at once she became insistent .... I had decided that I couldn't write any more out of Africa, and that what I wanted most was to return to my own people, my own land." The novel in her mind was *The Stone Angel*. The old woman, called Hagar, was its main character. "The novel poured forth," she said. "It was as if the old woman was actually there, telling me her life story."

Margaret, Jocelyn, David, and Jack, in Victoria, B.C., 1959.

Margaret, London, 1963.

ENGLAND

With this novel, Margaret's life took another path. She cared deeply for her husband, but she had to follow the gift of writing that had been given to her. In 1962, when Jack went off again to work on an engineering project, she did not go with him. She moved to England with her children, then ten and seven. It seemed to be a good place for a serious writer to work.

Soon, her books on Africa were being published both in England and in Canada. In 1964 *The Stone Angel* came out in New York, England, and Canada at the same time. This is the novel that launched Margaret Laurence as a writer of great importance. She had put into it her life, her heart, and her spirit. To this day it remains in print in countries all around the world.

ELM COTTAGE

For ten years the little family lived in a lovely old home called Elm Cottage. It was in the village of Penn in the English countryside. That was the house where Jocelyn and David grew up. That was the house where Margaret Laurence wrote six books. There was a large garden with roses and berry bushes. David built a tree house in one of the old apple trees. It was a homey place. Margaret wrote while the children were at school.

More stories from her prairie background were demanding to be written. *A Jest of God* tells the story of Rachel, 34, an unmarried school teacher. *The Fire-Dwellers* is the story of Rachel's sister Stacey, 39. Stacey is the mother of four children, with a husband who will not talk to her. *A Jest of God* won the Governor General's Award in 1966. Margaret travelled to Ottawa to receive it. *A Jest of God* was also made into a film.

Elm Cottage.

HOME TO CANADA

Canada seemed to be calling her home. She had many Canadian friends to stay with, but she needed a place to call her own. She bought a little cedar cottage on a river near Peterborough, Ontario. There she and the children spent the summers until Jocelyn and David finished school in England. The family called the cottage "The Shack". They loved their times there. A water-diviner was called to find the right place to drill a well in the yard. This seemed to be a magic gift to Margaret.

From this came the title *The Diviners* for the novel that was forming in her mind. At the shack, she wrote nearly all the time. A large sign on the door said, "No visitors between Monday and Friday. An important work is going on." It was put there by her publisher. He wanted the story as much as she did.

LAKEFIELD, ONTARIO

For two more years she worked on *The Diviners*, during the summers at the shack and the winters in England. But now she knew she wanted to move back to Canada. She found a lovely old two-storey brick house in Lakefield, Ontario. That was to be her home for the rest of her life. Again she won the Governor General's Award. Now Margaret Laurence was famous, much more famous than she ever wanted to be. She was made a Companion of the Order of Canada. She was also honoured by many universities.

Margaret at village grocery shop, Penn, Buckinghamshire,
1967.

Margaret moving into the Lakefield
House, 1974.

HER BOOKS

The Diviners was her last novel. Like *The Stone Angel*, *A Jest of God*, and *The Fire-Dwellers*, it was set in the town she called Manawaka. It was a town in Manitoba like the one where she was born. It is the story of Morag and her enduring love for a man not of her own race.

In all her books, Margaret Laurence created many memorable characters. In each of these novels, the main character is a woman. Each is a woman who cares, loves, hopes, and does the best she can with her life. Margaret Laurence was that kind of woman.

Among her books is a collection of short stories called *A Bird in the House*. The main character in the stories is called Vanessa, but the stories are really about Margaret herself. They tell of her growing-up years in the west.

Margaret Laurence died of cancer in 1987 at the age of 60. The last twelve years of her life were spent working and writing. They were also spent in speaking out for peace and justice, for a better role for women, and for clean air and water. During her last years, her daughter Jocelyn helped prepare her book of memoirs for publication. It is called *Dance on the Earth*. It was her final gift to us.

Louis J. Robichaud

by

Andrea Jeffery

Senate photo, 1991.

A MAN WITH A DREAM
FOR NEW BRUNSWICK

Before 1960 many Canadians thought New Brunswick was backward and poor. "Little Louis" Robichaud did a lot to change that image. On February 23, 1971 "The Transcript" said, "He changed the face of New Brunswick". "The Transcript" is a Moncton newspaper.

Louis J. Robichaud was Premier of New Brunswick from 1960 to 1970. Many people thought Louis Robichaud did a good job. But as they say, "You can't please all of the people all of the time." Many English-speaking people thought that Louis took from the English to give to the French.

That was not the way Louis saw it. His dream was to give all people in New Brunswick an equal chance for a good education and a good job.

A KENT BOY

Louis J. Robichaud was born on October 21, 1925 in Saint Antoine, Kent County, New Brunswick. He was the seventh child in a family of ten children. His father ran a small store and the post office. He also owned a small sawmill. Louis had a paper route. He helped to sort mail. He assisted in his father's store. When he grew older, he worked in his father's sawmill. Louis grew up in a happy family.

FAMILY POLITICS

The Robichaud family were proud to be Canadian but were also proud of their Acadian background. Acadians were the first settlers in what is now Nova Scotia and New Brunswick. They came from France and named their new home "Acadia".

Louis' family talked politics with neighbours and friends often. Most of them were Liberals. At that time the Premier of New Brunswick was a Liberal. The Prime Minister of Canada, William Lyon Mackenzie King, was also Liberal. When Louis was about nine years old, he started a scrapbook of political leaders. He was very interested in politics.

Louis' parents, then and in 1972.

SCHOOL

In school, Louis learned most things quickly but had trouble with English and math.

He was active in sports. After a snowfall, he would be the first to clean off the ice. He would then gather enough boys to play hockey.

When Louis was fifteen, he went to Bathurst to attend Sacré Coeur College. He joined a debating club and a political club. He also wrote for the student newspaper. Later, he became the editor of the paper. When Louis was about 18 years old, he decided that he wanted a political career. He wanted to be Premier of New Brunswick. In 1947 he graduated from Sacré Coeur College.

LOUIS GOES TO QUEBEC

From school in Bathurst he went to Laval University in Quebec City. He studied the economy and the social changes that followed World War Two. There were many young Acadians studying in Quebec. Louis believed they should return to New Brunswick when their studies were finished. They were needed to work for improvements in their province. In later years, Louis told some young people, "Plan your life with a purpose and you will be on the way to success." This was what he did.

BACK TO NEW BRUNSWICK

In 1949 Louis returned to New Brunswick. He wanted to be a lawyer but he did not have enough money to go to law school. Instead he worked in a law firm in Bathurst. At that time, it was possible to learn law by reading law books and having them explained by a lawyer.

1952—AN IMPORTANT YEAR

In 1952 Louis took his bar examinations—in English. He passed. Now he was a lawyer. He also got married that year. Louis and his wife Lorraine moved to Richibucto. Here Louis set up his own law office. He did not like all legal work but he enjoyed being in a courtroom. There he could use his debating skills. Louis and Lorraine thought alike on many things, including politics. His wife supported him in all his aims throughout his life.

In 1952 he also decided to run for the Liberals in northern Kent County. He travelled around Kent County. He talked about the need for better roads, new schools, and more jobs. He won.

THE OPPOSITION

In that same election, the Liberals were defeated. Conservative Hugh John Flemming became Premier of New Brunswick. Louis was part of the opposition. Now Louis worked hard, learning how government worked. He also worked on his English. During this time, he said that both the liquor laws and the education system needed to be improved.

LEADER OF THE LIBERAL PARTY

In the fall of 1958, Louis Robichaud became leader of the Liberal Party in his province. As Opposition Leader, there were many chances to complain about the Conservative government. Unemployment was rising. The government wanted to buy oil for the Power Commission plants. The Liberals said they should use local coal. The government did not want to open new mines.

There was a hospital tax of $50.00 per family, which the Conservative government had started. The Liberals said hospital expenses could be paid from the money the government had available. Flemming said there wasn't enough money to do this.

Robichaud making a speech.

THE 1960 ELECTION

Hugh John Flemming called an election for June 17, 1960. He thought he could win for sure. Louis and the Liberal Party ran mainly on the issue of the hospital insurance tax. Louis Robichaud said, "Elect me, and from the day I take office you shall cease to pay the hospital premium."

Louis travelled all over New Brunswick. Often his wife, Lorraine, went with him. In St. George, Louis was asked about re-opening moose hunting, which had been closed for twenty years. Louis agreed.

PREMIER OF NEW BRUNSWICK

K. C. Irving, another Kent boy, supported the Liberals during this election. He gave the Liberal Party a lot of money. Louis Robichaud won. At 34 years of age, he was the first Acadian to be elected Premier.

On that election day in 1960, no reporters were with Louis Robichaud in Richibucto. They did not think Robichaud would win. The news media have been careful never to let that happen with a leader again. They rushed to Richibucto to interview the new Acadian Premier. By 3 o'clock in the morning, there was a huge crowd outside the Robichaud home.

PREMIER

The Robichaud family moved to Fredericton. By then they had four children. They had to make new friends at their new schools. Lorraine Robichaud worried whether her English was good enough. As well, both Louis and Lorraine were very tired after all the work of the election. But the whole Robichaud family adjusted very well. Soon Lorraine was able to fill her role as hostess, wife, and mother.

The first thing Robichaud did was to cancel the hospital tax. The moose season was re-opened in a new way. There would be a draw every year. One thousand winners would be allowed to hunt moose each year.

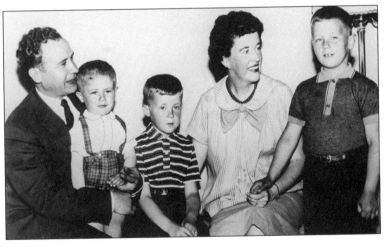

Robichaud, his wife and three of their children. The fourth child was born soon after.

CHANGES IN EDUCATION

Another committee studied education. Their report led to the building in 1963 of the Université de Moncton. This project used government money as well as gifts from the people. One English-speaking person who gave money was K. C. Irving. This was the first French-language university in New Brunswick. The university grew quickly. It has New Brunswick's first French language law school. It had a French language education program. One important result was that more Acadian students finished high school and went to university.

Robichaud enjoys a golf game at a Premiers' Conference.

COUNTY COUNCILS

A committee looked into local government and taxes. Robichaud started the program of "Equal Opportunity". This was his biggest dream. His plan was to give all people in New Brunswick equal government services.

Until now, county councils collected taxes. County councils supplied services when they could afford them. Therefore, lower income areas had less money for services. High income areas had better schools, hospitals, and social services.

In general, Acadian areas had lower incomes than other parts of the province. Thus they had lower standards of services. Some English-speaking areas also were very poor.

EQUAL OPPORTUNITY

"Equal Opportunity" raised living standards in all low income areas. The changes were very important for New Brunswick Acadians. French language schools now received support from the provincial government. Now there would be good schools in both languages. For most New Brunswickers, "Equal Opportunity" meant that the provincial government had more control over many services.

Many people didn't like "Equal Opportunity". Some people didn't like losing the county councils. In 1966 some people in Fredericton were very angry about "Equal Opportunity". There were threats on the Premier's life. When they were made public, they suddenly stopped.

SCHOOLS

"Equal Opportunity" made groups of small schools into one or two large schools. Before 1960 there were many schools in rural areas with only one or two rooms. Many of these had teachers who had no teacher training. The children did not have a chance to get a good education. Louis changed that.

Teacher training was improved. Salary levels were made equal across the province. More money was spent on education. This resulted in better teachers in rural areas. It meant better education for both Acadians and English in low income areas.

NEW BRUNSWICK FORESTS

An Italian firm wanted to get wood from New Brunswick. They told Robichaud they would build a mill in the Miramichi region. Robichaud wanted to help the Miramichi area. Robichaud had talked to K. C. Irving and other companies about building this mill. They said the market was not good enough then. So Robichaud decided to go with the Italian firm. He gave them a good deal. Irving was not happy about this. Louis lost his support. The Conservatives thought the government had given the Italian firm too much money. They argued so much that Louis said the people should decide. He called an election.

This tactic worked well for Robichaud. He won. Louis said this meant the people wanted him to get new industry. The mill did help the Miramichi region, but not as much as Robichaud had wanted.

Brunswick Mining and Smelting started mining in 1963. This mine, near Belledune, created jobs in the northeast. In 1965 a dam near Fredericton was begun. It employed over 3,000 people for over three years. It was opened in 1968.

Brunswick Mining and Smelting.

LANGUAGE

English was the only official language in New Brunswick. In July 1969 Louis Robichaud began the work of changing New Brunswick's laws. French and English would have equal status in schools, courts, government agencies, and the legislature. In the 1970's Richard Hatfield finished that work. New Brunswick became a bilingual province.

THE 1970 ELECTION

In 1970 there was still anger and bad feeling over "Equal Opportunity". Richard Hatfield was leader of the Conservatives. His main idea for the election was, "We need a change". Richard Hatfield won. Hatfield knew that much of "Equal Opportunity" was needed. He also knew that New Brunswick needed to have two official languages. He would not undo the improvements Louis had made.

Lorraine and Louis Robichaud.

AFTER 1970

After his defeat, Louis Robichaud became the chairman of the International Joint Commission. Here he helped New Brunswick with hydro resources and pollution control matters. He did not enjoy this work. It also took him away from home too much.

In December 1973 Louis Robichaud became a Senator. At 48 he was the youngest member of the Senate. He and his wife Lorraine now live near Ottawa. There he represents the interests of New Brunswick in the Senate.

Mr. Robichaud also became active with the Kidney Foundation of Canada. He had lost one son because of kidney problems. Often he spoke to chapters of the Foundation across Canada. He became interested in kidney research.

Another son, Paul, graduated in business administration and law. He now works in the Department of Finance in Ottawa. Another son, René, graduated in business administration from Harvard University and works in New York City. Their daughter, Monique, is now married and lives near Louis and Lorraine in Ottawa.

HOBBIES

Louis has always enjoyed golf and wood-working. He has the patience both these hobbies need. When he was Premier, sometimes he would be in his workshop most of the night. He found wood-working very relaxing. He still likes to "turn wood" today. He has many books on wood-working. He makes all kinds of furniture, including cabinets, tables, and table lamps.

LITTLE LOUIS—BIG DREAMS

Louis had a dream. It was that New Brunswick could be more modern. French and English should have equal chances for education and good jobs. English and French could live side by side in the province. They could live together in peace and happiness.

Louis Robichaud will always be remembered for his reforms in education. In those days, people didn't talk about literacy. But today we know literacy is important. We now see that "Little Louis" Robichaud helped to improve literacy in New Brunswick.

One of Louis' dreams: The Mactaquac Dam.

Premier Robichaud receives an honorary degree from
Cardinal Léger, Archbishop of Montreal and Chancellor of
the University of Montreal, 1961.

Emily Carr
Canada's Famous Artist

by
Michael Collins

Emily Carr was born on March 3, 1871 in Victoria, British Columbia, the youngest of five daughters. Her father, Richard Carr, left England in 1837. He led an adventurous life. He found gold in the 1849 California gold rush. Later, he had several successful stores near San Francisco. After his marriage he sold his business in the United States. He and his wife returned to England. They did not like living there. In 1863 they returned to North America. They went to live in Victoria on Vancouver Island. Carr started a wholesale business and built a big home.

The Carr Homestead.

EMILY'S CHILDHOOD IN VICTORIA.

The year Emily was born, British Columbia became a province of the new Dominion of Canada. Life was different in the 1870s. There were no telephones or electric power. Water for homes came from wells or cisterns. Tall trees crowded in on the small city. There was an Indian Reserve near Victoria's harbour.

Emily was a lively child. The Carr home was orderly and strict. Emily rebelled at times. She was not like her milder, older sisters nor her younger brother, Dick. She became interested in the Native people and their way of life. Her family thought this was not proper for a young girl.

From her father Emily learned a great deal about nature. The Carrs had a large garden and a small barn on their property. They kept a cow, pigs, chickens, and other small birds and animals. Beacon Hill Park was near the Carr home. The family often went to the park. Emily developed a lasting interest in the outdoors.

As a young girl, Emily showed skill in drawing. She took lessons at school and from a private teacher.

EMILY, THE ORPHAN

When Emily was twelve years old, her mother died. Two years later her father died. Emily's eldest sister, Edith, became the head of the Carr household. Emily spent some time away from the Carr home. She stayed with family friends named Green.

Richard Carr left a small fortune to his children. A family friend looked after their property and money.

The Carr sisters.

EMILY GOES TO SAN FRANCISCO

Making money was more important than art in Victoria. There was no place in Victoria where Emily could develop her artistic skills.

Emily wanted more training. Her sisters and the family guardian did not agree. They did not think that a young woman could earn a living as an artist. Emily persisted. They finally agreed that she could go to San Francisco. There she would attend the California School of Design. Emily could stay with friends there. In 1890, when she was nineteen, Emily sailed from Victoria.

She was not happy in San Francisco. She found fault with the friends with whom she lived. She found fault with her teachers. She was only happy when sketching and painting out-of-doors. The School of Design did improve her skills in art. She learned a great deal about painting portraits, still life, and landscapes. She studied sketching and water colour painting.

SHE OPENS A STUDIO

Emily returned to Victoria in 1893. She had a studio in the loft of the barn on the family property. She taught art to children. She enjoyed working with children. She enjoyed it most when she took the children to Beacon Hill to sketch outdoors.

Emily found time to do some of her own art work. Victoria, in the 1890s, did not have an art museum nor an art society. But the annual Fall Fair had an art exhibit for the work of local artists. At the Fair, Emily won first prize in 1894 and 1895.

NATIVE PEOPLES IN EMILY'S ART

In the 1890s, Emily painted what she saw. In the summer months she began to go on sketching and painting trips along the west coast of Vancouver Island. Her art began to include Native people. Her work showed how the Native people lived.

One of Emily's pictures of a native village.

EMILY GOES TO ENGLAND

Emily still wanted more training. In 1899 she went to England. She entered the Westminster School of Art in London.

Emily's course of studies in London was for two years. Most of the teaching was indoors. Working inside a building depressed her. She injured her foot. She had to have an operation to remove a toe. It took a few months for her to recover from this operation. The death of her brother, Dick, also upset her.

During the summer months, Westminster School of Art closed. Emily sketched and painted happily in the country away from London.

ST. IVES

When her course finished, Emily moved to the small village of St. Ives in Cornwall. This is on the southwest coast of England. There Emily gained skill in the use of lighting in her seascape paintings. She also painted in the woods near St. Ives. Light, she found, shone in the darkest parts of the forest. She studied at St. Ives for eight months.

BUSHEY

Next, she moved to Bushey not far from London. At Bushey she painted mostly in water-colours.

Emily's health had been troublesome in London. At Bushey she became very sick. She was put in a hospital in Suffolk. She stayed there for eighteen months. When she recovered, she returned to Bushey to study. She wanted to go home to Canada. It was, however, several months before she was strong enough to travel. She had been in England for five years. Emily thought that her long stay in England had not been a success. But she had gained more knowledge and skills than she realized.

RETURN TO CANADA

When she returned she spent several weeks in the Cariboo country of British Columbia. She stayed with a friend from her girlhood days, Edna Green. The weeks in the Cariboo were fun for Emily. She loved the beautiful scenery of forest and mountains.

When she returned to Victoria, Emily worked on a local newspaper. She drew political cartoons. The next year, 1906, she moved to Vancouver. She opened a studio and taught art to children again. This was a happy time for her.

Emily made a very important friend, Sophie Frank, at this time. Sophie was a basket maker from a North Vancouver Indian Reserve. They spent many happy times together. They remained friends until Sophie died, years later. Emily thought that her paintings of native life were a tribute to Sophie.

THE ALASKA TRIP

The next year, Emily and her sister Alice travelled to Alaska. For the first time Emily saw native totem poles in their village settings. She decided to do paintings of these totems. She felt that her art would be a record of native life and beliefs. The villages were on the British Columbia mainland and the Queen Charlotte Islands. For several years she made trips to these villages. There she painted and sketched. She captured a very important part of Canada's history.

During these years, Emily was busy teaching. She showed her paintings at regional art shows. The totem pole paintings gave Emily recognition as an artist. She still thought something was missing from her work.

TO FRANCE

Emily wanted to go to France. She had heard of a new style of painting. It was called "Impressionism". This style was less concerned with form and detail. The artist tries to capture in paint the impression of what the eye sees in life.

Emily had saved enough money to go to France to study. In the summer of 1910 she and her sister Alice left Victoria for France.

Emily enrolled in a famous art academy. Because she was working indoors at the academy, again she became sick. Emily and Alice then went to Sweden. There Emily got better.

Emily, later in her career with one of her pictures in the background.

BACK TO FRANCE

They returned to France. Emily went to northern Brittany. She sketched and painted in the country and villages. Two of her paintings were accepted for an art exhibition in Paris.

The work Emily did in Paris and Brittany was different. It was a drastic change for her. Emily went from the representational painting to the new style very quickly.

THE VANCOUVER EXHIBITION

When she returned home, Emily opened a studio in Vancouver. She exhibited her Brittany paintings. Few people came to see them. Vancouver people were only mildly interested in this new way of painting. Nor did she get many students. Few people wanted to paint using this new style.

During the summer she was able to take a sketching trip. She went along the British Columbia coast and to the Queen Charlotte Islands. She returned to Vancouver with a great many sketches and drawings.

Emily did not have much money. Few of the totem pole paintings had sold. Nor had the years treated the Carr fortune kindly. Investments turned out poorly.

At this time, there was talk that the provincial government was considering the establishment of an art gallery. Emily offered her collection of totem pole paintings. The offer was refused by the province. The refusal hurt her. She decided she could not afford to stay in Vancouver.

EMILY: LANDLADY

The Carr family decided to divide their property into lots. Each sister kept one lot and the rest were sold. Emily borrowed money and had an apartment house built on her lot. She planned to use the rental income from two of the apartments for her expenses. She would live and work in the other apartment.

World War One began. New laws kept rents low. Emily did not have enough money for her expenses. To get extra money, she hooked rugs, made pottery and raised dogs for sale. Emily went downtown in Victoria every day. She pushed a wicker pram to carry home the food for her dogs and pets. Some of her dogs, cats, and Woo, her pet monkey, went with her. Her neighbours saw this parade every day. They decided Emily was odd. This work and caring for her tenants took a lot of energy. She had little time or the desire to paint.

Emily and her animals.

THE LONELY ARTIST

For years Emily worked mostly alone. But her paintings of totem poles became known outside her home province. In 1927 the National Gallery of Canada chose some of her paintings for their Canadian West Coast Art Exhibition. Emily travelled to Ottawa to see this successful exhibition. Her paintings were well received.

She also visited Toronto. This time she met some of the artists known as the Group of Seven. They had some of Emily's work. They thought her west coast paintings were similar to the work they were doing.

These artists painted in a style and in colours that expressed their feelings about what they painted. The Group were painting Canadian landscapes in a style that Emily had not seen before. Emily admired their work. She knew she could use this style in her own paintings.

Lawren Harris, one of the artists in the Group of Seven, thought Emily was a skilled and remarkable painter. Emily, in turn, liked Harris's paintings. His encouragement helped Emily. She overcame the self-doubts that she had about herself as an artist.

EMILY RETURNS TO PAINTING

When Emily returned to Victoria, she began to paint again. The years of very little painting, from 1913 to 1927, were over. She took a long sketching and painting trip up the coast of British Columbia. She visited the Queen Charlotte Islands again. She came back with many sketches. These were turned into paintings later.

At this time, the noted American artist Mark Tobey visited Victoria. Emily learned much from him. Tobey helped her see how light and shade could be used with good effect in her paintings.

Lawren Harris and Emily wrote letters about art. He suggested that she should include the forests and mountains in her paintings. Emily started to paint as Harris suggested. Her work began to express how she felt about what she painted.

Emily had used many different materials in her art. Now, as she painted powerful canvasses of forests, mountains, skies, and seascapes, she used oils.

The once lonely artist was beginning to receive recognition for her work. The art world now saw Emily Carr as a painter of power and originality. World centres began to show her work at art exhibitions.

In British Columbia she continued her sketching and painting of the forest and mountains.

A NEW STUDIO

Emily sold her apartment house. She went to stay with Alice. She had a small room for a studio. All the chairs in her studio were raised to the ceiling. This was done with small ropes and pulleys. She said it gave her more room to paint. It also gave her more control over visitors. If she didn't want them to stay, the chairs remained up on the ceiling. If she liked a visitor, she would lower a chair.

HOUSE TRAILER

Her trips had always taken a great deal of energy. Emily was growing old. She needed some comfort on her trips. She bought a small house trailer and had it towed to where she wanted to work. It was her sketching and painting base for the next four years.

Emily and friends at house trailer.

SICKNESS STRIKES AGAIN

In 1937 Emily had a heart attack. Her doctor would not let her paint. Earlier she had taken a correspondence course on short-story writing. This now proved helpful. During the years Emily had kept diaries about her sketching trips. She now turned to them for material and wrote stories. Most of her stories were about the Native people of her province. The stories were read over the radio. People liked them. They became part of her first book, *Klee Wyck*. It won the Governor General's Award for non-fiction.

At the same time, there were successful exhibitions of her paintings in Vancouver and in England. Successes in both art and writing helped her to recover her health. She spent a few years writing other successful books.

But the excitement of the acceptance of her art and her literary activity was cut short. She suffered another heart attack. This was a serious one. Emily did not give up easily. Her struggles throughout the years had steeled her to fight. She recovered enough to go back to sketching again. It was only for a short time. She had another heart attack. On March 2, 1945, at Victoria, Emily Carr died. Alice was the only Carr left to mourn her passing.

EMILY CARR, ARTIST AND WRITER

Emily Carr overcame great odds to become an artist. She became Emily Carr, Canada's most original and famed woman artist. She became Emily Carr, famous artist, respected world wide. She also became Emily Carr, world famous and renowned writer.

Armand Bombardier
Inventor of the Snowmobile

by

Bernice Cleator

THE FIRST SNOWMOBILE

It was a quiet afternoon in the village of Valcourt, Quebec. It was Christmas holiday time in 1922. The few village cars were all up on blocks for the winter. Nothing could travel on the roads but horse-pulled sleighs. As it did every year, the deep snow had cut off the village.

Suddenly the winter quiet was shattered. A strange machine roared down the main street. Horses reared, people ran for shelter, and great clouds of snow flew everywhere. What was it? An airplane? A sleigh? A car? No one could say. It had parts of all three.

The machine was the world's first snowmobile. Its inventor was a boy of 15, named Armand Bombardier.

World's first snowmobile.

HIS BOYHOOD

Joseph-Armand, called Armand, was born on April 16, 1907. His parents farmed near the village of Valcourt. He was the first of eight children. As a boy, he liked most of all to get into his father's wood-working shop on the farm. Here repairs were made to farm machines: tractors, threshers, and wood-cutting machines. It soon became clear that the young Armand had a way with machines. He could get them to work when no one else could. He had, they said, a magic touch. But farm life was hard.

MOVE TO VALCOURT

When Armand was 13, his family moved into the village. His parents wanted a better life for their children. They bought the Valcourt General Store. Now Armand could make a bit of money delivering goods from the store after school. For five cents a week he also helped with the Masses in his church.

Armand was always inventing things. On the farm he had been able to pick up bits and pieces to use for his inventions. He had made toy boats and trains for his little brothers. He had even built a tractor with an engine that worked. But now, in the village, he had to save his money to buy parts.

First he went to see the watch repair man. From a box of old parts, he bought tiny levers and wheels and springs. From large clocks he got larger motors. With one of these, he made a motor boat that chugged down the river nearby. His friends cheered.

The tractor Armand made for his little brothers.

ARMAND'S STEAM ENGINE

Soon everyone in the village knew Armand and his inventions. One was a small cannon that went off with a great roar, scaring everyone. Joseph-Armand studied the locomotives at the Valcourt train station. Then he decided to build his own steam engine. When he had worked on the plans, he built the engine with the help of a friend. He used an air pump and parts from an old sewing machine.

Three mechanics were in town to repair the church's heating system. They were interested in Joseph-Armand's engine. So they invited him to try it out on the church's steam system. The small engine ran for a moment but blew up under the pressure. Joseph-Armand was pleased because his engine had actually worked. It was a close call, but no one was hurt, only shaken up.

HIS EARLY TRAINING

The Bombardier parents and children were devout Roman Catholics. Armand's father wanted his first son to be a priest. At 14 Armand was sent off to the seminary in the city of Sherbrooke, about 50 kilometres away. There he studied Latin, Greek, and math, but his heart was not in it. Armand loved his church, but he wanted to be a mechanic, not a priest. It was during his Christmas holiday from the seminary that Armand built his first snowmobile. It had an engine from an old car, runners from a farm sleigh, and a propeller carved by the boy himself. And it went!

After two years at the seminary, Armand won over his father. At the age of 16, he began his real training. First, he worked as an apprentice mechanic at a garage in a village nearby. Then he went to Montreal to work as a mechanic. At night he took courses in mechanics and electricity. He read everything he could get his hands on.

ARMAND'S DREAM

Armand still had his dream.The winters in Quebec were long and snowy. Everything came to a stop. He wanted to beat the snow. He wanted to invent something that could ride over it. He knew that in other northern countries inventors were working to make machines that would do that. So far, none worked well. Far northern areas still had only snow-shoes or dog-sleds for getting around in the long snowy winter.

With many dreams and plans in his head, Armand returned to Valcourt. He was 19. He was ready to begin his career. His father built a garage for him in the village. There he repaired and sold cars. He also repaired all kinds of motors and machines for the farmers in the area. He was able to hire his uncle, his brother, and his brother-in-law.

But winter was a quiet time. The cars were all up on blocks, and the farm machines were stored in barns. Now, Armand could get to work on his snowmobile ideas.

THE SECOND SNOWMOBILE

His second snowmobile was a car with extra wheels at the back. Belts were placed around these wheels to grip the snow. The front wheels were taken off and replaced with runners like skis. Armand drove this machine around the village, to the delight of the people. But when spring came, cars and farm machines were able to move, and Armand's snowmobile plans had to be set aside.

As the winter of 1927 set in, Armand got back to his snow car. He built a new one, bigger and better than the last. The hotel owner bought it to pick up his customers from the train. It was much more comfortable than an open sleigh. Over the next few years, Armand kept improving this model. He always started with a car, replacing the wheels with skis. He sold a dozen of these. Doctors and vets liked them for making their rounds in the winter.

Armand was a very busy man. Sometimes he was hidden under a truck. Or he might be in his tiny office, doing his accounts or drawing plans for improving his snowmobile.

Snow Car, 1927.

MARRIAGE

Armand had little spare time, but he began to date the sister of one of his employees.

In 1929, at the age of 22, Armand married Yvonne Labrecque. They had six children.

MORE SNOWMOBILES

By 1933 he had invented two more snowmobiles. This time he did not use a car. Instead, he built bodies of plywood and canvas, put them on four skis, and drove them by propeller. Armand always tested his new models himself. Often they let him down, and he had to walk back to the garage through the deep snow.

In the winter of 1934, all his snow cars lay in pieces on the floor of his garage. He was trying to invent a better model. At that time his little two-year-old son suddenly became ill. The doctor said he must be taken to the hospital in Sherbrooke at once. Armand did not have a snow car in working order, and the roads were blocked by snow. Within hours the little boy died.

SNOWMOBILE FACTORY

Now Armand was more determined than ever to beat the snows of winter. Sometimes he worked all through the night. By 1935 he had invented a model that was the beginning of his snowmobile factory. It was his most important invention so far. He and his workers built six more of these. People lined up to buy them. Now Armand had no time to sell and repair cars. He changed the name of his garage to "L'Auto-Neige BBO", a snowmobile factory.

In 1937 the factory turned out the B7 (B for Bombardier; 7 because it could carry seven people). Most of these were sold to doctors, funeral directors, priests, milkmen, mailmen, woodsmen, and salesmen of all kinds.

B12s (to carry 12 people) followed soon after. Orders came in every day. B12s were used as school buses. They carried children over deep winter snow to little country schools.

The first factory, "L'Auto-Niege BBO".

THE WAR, 1939-1945

Then came the war. In the six war years, the Bombardier factory built five different kinds of troop carriers for the Canadian government. One of these, called the B1, had no skis but had big wheels on each side with a rubber belt around them, a sprocket wheel at the front, and a wide track. Many were used in the snowy fields of Norway.

Then Bombardier's most important war machine came out. It carried two people — a driver and a soldier. It had openings for guns and a lookout hatch on top. It was built to go anywhere. It was used in the swamps of Italy and in the South Pacific war areas. It was also used for military tests in the Canadian Arctic. Even at 40 degrees below zero it started right up.

At the end of the war, production of the B12 started up again. They were sold with great success.

By 1948 the roads of Quebec were being cleared by snowplows. Now cars could travel in winter. There was not so much need for snowmobiles.

A new idea — the Muskeg Tractor

SEARCH FOR NEW IDEAS

Armand was looking for new ideas. He travelled all across Canada. He watched lumbermen at work. He watched oil workers. Both had to work in swampy, soggy land called muskeg. Muskeg covers much of northern Canada. Armand went back to his planning in Valcourt. By 1953 he had invented a new, flexible sprocket wheel and a vulcanizing apparatus which enabled him to make endless rubber tracks. These two new inventions gave birth to the Muskeg Tractor. This was one of his most important inventions. Orders came in from all over the world. The Muskeg Tractor was used by oil workers, telephone line workers, Hydro workers, road and railway builders, woodsmen, and others.

Armand beside the "Muskeg"

THE SKI-DOO

Now Armand Bombardier was a very rich man. His factory employed many people. But nothing changed. He worked as hard as ever, and he kept on inventing.

He had always dreamed of building a small vehicle that could carry one or two people over deep snow. One of his goals was to replace the dog-sled in the far north.

In 1957 engines were getting small. This made it possible for him to work on his dream. This machine became his Ski-Dog. By train and airplane he travelled 800 kilometres north of Montreal to test it. The Native peoples hailed it. It would open up a whole new way of life for them. Back in Valcourt, he set his factory humming. 225 Ski-Dogs were built in 1959.

According to a story, a typing error changed the "g" to "o". From this came the name Ski-Doo. This new name was received with great favour. So it was adopted.

He always knew that the Ski-Doo could be used for fun as well as work. Armand Bombardier had not only invented a new machine; he had invented a new sport! He himself loved to race his Ski-Doo over the snow. He loved to give his wife and children rides under the stars. He enjoyed competing with others.

In 1963 L'Auto-Neige Bombardier filled 8,000 orders for Ski-Doos. The company employed 380 workers. Most of Armand's brothers were in the company. Many of the people of Valcourt also worked there. Armand was very proud of them all.

Great wealth and success still failed to change him. His working hours were as long as ever. Honours came his way. The University of Sherbrooke named one of its buildings after him.

"Muskeg" in use in arctic conditions.

UNTIMELY DEATH

But that same year, Armand's health began to fail. In 1964 he died of cancer. He was 56. He was buried in the cemetery behind the church he attended all his life.

One year after his death, in 1965, his family wished to continue his charitable work. They set up a foundation in his name. His wife and daughters took charge of it. Donations go to different charities. The young people of Valcourt and its region are also given help in getting an education.

THE MUSEUM

Today you can visit the J.-Armand Bombardier Museum in the village of Valcourt. To reach it, you drive south-east of Montreal. You enter Valcourt by the same road Armand used when he scared the villagers with his first snowmobile. The museum shows two kinds of exhibits. One is about J.-Armand Bombardier. Here you can see the machines invented by Armand. His old garage is part of the museum. The second exhibit shows the international history of the making of the small snowmobile.

BOMBARDIER INC.

It all began with a boy and his dream. But it did not end with his death. The company was taken over by his son-in-law. L'Auto-Neige Bombardier became Bombardier Inc. Today, Armand's youngest son is vice-chairman. There are employees in countries including Canada, U.S.A., France, Belgium, Austria, and Great Britain.

Bombardier Inc. builds railway cars, subway trains, and high speed trains. It built the Monorail at Disney World in Florida. Now it is building the rail cars for the new underwater tunnel between England and France. The corporation owns aircraft companies. It also builds the water bombers for dropping water on forest fires. It has moved into space and has built rockets and missiles. Sea-Doos, made for travel over water, are another invention.

What would Armand Bombardier think of this great company that he started in his garage? He would probably go on inventing. He would go on helping the people of Valcourt and many other places.

The Bombardier family

René Lévesque

by

Freda Hudson

René Lévesque was born in 1922. He died in 1987. After his death, an important street in Montreal was given his name. The name of the street was changed from Dorchester to René Lévesque Boulevard. The Province of Quebec wanted to honour him. He had helped to make many changes in the province. He was well known and well loved.

THE FAMILY

He was born in a hospital in Campbellton in New Brunswick. But his home was New Carlisle in Quebec. New Carlisle is on the coast of the Gaspé peninsula. It looks out towards the sea. It looks towards New Brunswick and Prince Edward Island. It was built by English-speaking settlers. Many of the first settlers came from the Channel Islands. Many years ago, the Channel Islands had belonged to the French. The settlers had French names, but they spoke English.

René, aged three.

HISTORY

René's family had a long history. The history of the Lévesque family goes back to the 17th century. At that time, Robert Lévesque married Jeanne Chevalier. René was a direct descendent of that marriage. The language of the Lévesque family was French. His mother and father had lived in Rivière-du-Loup. His father's name was Dominique Lévesque. His mother was Diane Dionne. Rivière-du-Loup is a city on the south shore of the St. Lawrence River. It is north of Quebec City. It is many miles away from New Carlisle.

René's parents moved from Rivière-du-Loup to New Carlisle. Dominique Lévesque was a lawyer. They moved when René's father joined a law office. He joined the law office of John Hall Kelly, an Irish-Canadian. Dominique had wanted to go into politics. He was a Liberal. His idol was Sir Wilfrid Laurier. Politics is a tiring job and Dominique was not strong enough. He had suffered an attack of Spanish 'flu. Politics would have been too hard on his health.

LIFE IN NEW CARLISLE

René grew up speaking two languages, English and French. English was the language of the streets in New Carlisle. Children in the Catholic school were taught in English.

Dominique Lévesque did very well in New Carlisle. He owned one of the first cars in the town. John Hall Kelly was the godfather of Dominique's first child, René.

"A DIFFICULT CHILD"

René admitted that he was a "difficult child". He remembered being tied by his left ankle to the porch railing. This was to prevent him from going near the edge of the water. It also stopped him from stealing matches. He remembered burning down a fence. Luckily, the barn did not burn down too.

His parents sent him to visit his grandparents. His grandfather ran a general store in Rivière-du-Loup. René's memories of the times with his grandparents were happy. He remembered playing cards with his grandmother and her friends. The card games were usually poker!

There was no electricity in his home. He learned the alphabet by oil lamp. He learned on his father's knee from a big red book. The house was crowded with books.

THE SCHOOL YEARS

René's first school was a one-room school house. It was a kilometre from his home. A kilometre was a long way for a little boy to walk. René wrote, "On certain winter days, with a blizzard whipping my face, I would walk all the way backwards." Here he learned to count, to write, to speak, and to read.

His father was not happy with the one-room school. He knew that his son was very clever. He wanted the best schooling for him. At age eleven René was sent to boarding school in Gaspé. The town of Gaspé is on the tip of the Gaspé peninsula.

When René arrived at the school, the first thing he asked to see was the library.

Dominique Lévesque died when René was fourteen. He died in the hospital in Campbellton. It was the same hospital where René had been born.

After his father's death, his mother moved the family to Quebec city. René's education continued. He went to a French-language college. Then he attended Laval University in Quebec City.

At the Gaspé school he was known as a brilliant student. When he went to the Jesuit college in Quebec City he was still considered to be brilliant. He had a very good memory. He found school easy until he reached university. Because learning had been easy for him, he had not learned good study habits. He found law school dull.

At the end of 1943 René was 21 years old. He had become a poor student. He skipped lectures and played cards. He spent too much time going to movies.

Lévesque during his student days.

RENÉ AND WORLD WAR II

The Second World War was still being fought. Because he was now failing his courses, he was in danger of being drafted into the Canadian Army. He didn't want to go into the army. To avoid that he went to Montreal. Then he went to New York. He was looking for some way to avoid being drafted. He wanted to go overseas to the war zones. But he did not want to go as a soldier. In New York he was offered a job. The job was in the French language service of the United States Office of War Information. He was sent overseas. Early in 1944 he sailed from Montreal. He worked in the London radio studios. He wrote scripts and read reports. He was broadcasting to the French-speaking people in Belgium. He was broadcasting also to northern France.

SENIOR WAR CORRESPONDENT

René was sent to the European continent to report on the advance of the U.S. forces. He also acted as liaison officer between American and French officers. His two languages made this job easy. In the spring of 1945 he was assigned as senior correspondent to the U.S. Seventh Army. During the closing months of the war René went through Alsace. He went into Germany, through Bavaria and into Austria. He was with the first Americans to enter Dachau. Dachau was a German concentration camp. René described it as "hell on earth".

René was preparing to go to the Pacific war zone. But the atomic bomb ended the war with Japan. Early in 1946 he was back in Montreal.

THE CANADIAN BROADCASTING CORPORATION

On his return to Quebec, René thought of working in the United States. It was easier, however, to accept an offer to join the CBC. He was now a married man. In 1947 he had married Louise L'Heureux. They had two sons, Pierre and Claude. Later, a third child was born. His third child was a daughter, Suzanne.

He worked in the French-language section of the CBC. This had been started in 1943. In 1951 he was sent by Radio-Canada to cover the Korean War. In 1953 he went to England to report on the coronation of Queen Elizabeth II. Two years later he was in the Soviet Union with Lester B. Pearson. Pearson was, at that time, Minister of External Affairs. Later, Pearson was Prime Minister of Canada.

FRENCH LANGUAGE TELEVISION

The French language television service of the CBC began in Quebec in 1952. René played an important role in those early days.

The French-language television service changed French Quebec forever. Small communities were able to see a wider world. René was an important figure. He was the host of a TV program. The program was called "Point de Mire" (Point of View). It was a public affairs program. René would explain world events in front of a blackboard in the TV studio. He became a familiar and loved figure. Surrounded by cigarette smoke and chalk dust, he reached out to the people. Both French and English admired his simple style. He spoke to everyone. But most of all he was a friend of the people.

ON STRIKE

On December 22, 1958, 74 French-language radio and TV producers voted to strike. The issue   at the heart of the strike was the right to form a union. By the time the 69-day strike was ended, René had discovered the politics of nationalism. The government in Ottawa was not sympathetic. At this time, the Conservative party was in power. Also, there was not much support from the English-speaking producers in the national broadcasting system.

René was put in jail as a result of the strike. Here he is coming out of jail.

RENÉ ENTERS POLITICS

After the strike, René returned to the CBC. But he didn't stay long. He was now interested in provincial politics. He became a candidate for the Liberal party in the 1960 election. The Liberals won the election. René became a provincial cabinet member. He had no political experience, but he learned quickly. He thought that the hydro-electric system should be owned by the province. In 1962 he succeeded in this aim. He had been in politics only two years!

During the years he spent with the Liberals he worked very hard. He served as Minister of Natural Resources. Later he was Minister of Family and Welfare.

René with Inuit when Minister of Natural Resources.

THE LIBERALS LOSE AN ELECTION

In 1963 René had been less than three years in politics. By then he had become very important. Next to Premier Lesage, he was thought to be the most powerful man in the party. It seemed that he would be the future leader of the Liberal Party in Quebec. In 1966 the Liberals lost the election. They were beaten by the Union Nationale.

The news that the Union Nationale was again in power stunned the country. When in power before, their government had been very dishonest. The Liberals had fought hard to clean up the government. The loss of the election stunned Canada, but it also stunned the Liberal party.

RENÉ FOUNDS A NEW PARTY

In 1967 René left the Liberal party. His ideas were not shared by the Liberals. When he left the party he also left many friends. Robert Bourassa told reporters that Lévesque's leaving was a "great loss for the party. It will be difficult to replace him."

He founded a separatist party. René once said that he had moved toward separatism "bit by bit—without even noticing." The party he founded joined with another group. They became the Parti Québécois (Quebec Party). At that time he believed that independence was the answer. He believed that Quebec should separate from Canada. He believed that Quebec should control its own economy. He believed that French-Canadians were being treated unfairly.

INDEPENDENCE FOR QUEBEC

The idea of independence for Quebec is not new. It dates back to before the rebellion of 1837. That rebellion was a failure, but the idea of independence did not die. The idea was always there. Any time there was a crisis in Quebec, thoughts of independence would come alive again. There was a crisis during the First World War. The crisis was over conscription. People in Quebec did not want to be forced to fight a war. During the 1920's and 30's interest in separation was high. The question of conscription during the Second World War was again a crisis.

THE SEPARATISTS IN POWER

Nine years later René was proved to be right. In 1976 the Parti Québécois won the election. They won against the Liberal government of Robert Bourassa. René's Parti Québécois government tried to correct many wrongs. He wanted a democratic society. He wanted a society with justice for everyone. Although his ideas were not shared by all P.Q. members, he changed the face of Quebec politics.

RENÉ WANTED A "YES" VOTE

In 1980, due to pressure inside the party, Lévesque held a referendum. It was a proposal to give authority to government leaders to negotiate with the Canadian government. The discussions would be for independence for Quebec. René was heartbroken when the answer was NO. The NO vote was from the people of Quebec. They had refused to consider the idea of separation. But in 1981 the people of Quebec elected René again.

René was upset when the vote was "NO".

DEFEAT

In 1982-83 Lévesque tried to reduce public spending. This was fought by the unions. The Lévesque government was losing its popularity.

In 1985 René seemed to give up dreams of independence. He was working more to develop a better economy for Quebec. He and hard-line separatists disagreed. He resigned as party leader later that year. The hard-line separatists had beaten him. But the separatists themselves were also defeated. At the next election, the Liberal party won. Robert Bourassa was once again the Premier of Quebec. The Parti Québécois was still fighting for independence.

DEATH OF RENÉ LÉVESQUE

René died in 1987. He did not see his dream for Quebec come true. He is still loved by many people in Quebec, both English- and French-speaking. He is loved even by those who did not share his dream. He was a hard-working, honest man. He worked hard for what he believed. While in office he made changes in the automobile insurance plan. This gave greater protection to the victims of accidents. His government also banned secret funding for elections.

René Lévesque Boulevard is a reminder of the man who made a long trip from the little town in the Gaspé. That trip led him to power and fame! He will live on in the history of Canada.

Kenojuak

By

Gladys E. Neale

The Inuit are native Canadians who live in the far north of our country. Many are famous for their carvings of animals and their way of life. One who is known the world over for her skills in art is Kenojuak. This is her story.

CHILDHOOD

In the far north, when the land was already frozen over, Kenojuak was born. It was the autumn of 1927. Kenojuak remembers crossing the Hudson Strait in a small boat when she was a young child. Her family was moving from Cape Dorset. They moved to northern Quebec. In that place the Inuit hunted and trapped the polar bear. They also hunted other wild animals such as the fox. They sold their furs to the Hudson's Bay Company.

MURDER IN THE CAMP

Kenojuak loved her father. He was a kind and generous man. Often he gave food to those Inuit who did not have enough. In spite of this, many of the Inuit in the area feared Kenojuak's father.

During the winter of 1933 there were disagreements over the value of furs. Perhaps Kenojuak's father was part of these quarrels. One winter's day will always remain in Kenojuak's mind. Her father left their snowhouse to go hunting. The family heard shots. They ran to him but he was already dead. Three men had waited to kill him. Then they tied rocks to his neck, wrists, and ankles.

The body was thrown into the sea. Everything he owned was also thrown into the sea. Some of his dogs were shot, but some ran away into the hills. They were never seen again.

These acts may seem strange to some people. The Inuit tried to maintain peace in their camps. Everyone had to obey the rules of the camp. Anyone who did not obey the rules was made to suffer. A man was chosen, or perhaps several, to deal with someone who did wrong. Sometimes this resulted in more killings when the family wanted revenge. Perhaps Kenojuak's father did not follow the rules of his group. His death was thus decided.

For the rest of that winter the family suffered and often went hungry. In the spring they returned to Cape Dorset.

Cape Dorset.

INUIT WAY OF LIFE

As Kenojuak grew up she lived the Inuit way of life. Her home was in camps along the southern coast of Baffin Island.

The Arctic char is part of the food of the Inuit. Char is quite like salmon. When the fish swim into the lakes, the Inuit catch them. They wade into the icy waters. They use long handled, three-pronged spears to catch the char. Kenojuak learned to clean, split, and dry the fish in the air. She worked with the other women in the camp. The char was then stored for eating in the winter months. For their dogs, whole fish were tossed into large stone storage places.

LEARNING TO READ

Kenojuak learned to read the Book of Common Prayer. This is printed in the Inuit language. When Kenojuak was young this was the only book they had to read.

MARRIAGE

As Kenojuak approached womanhood, a marriage was made for her. She did not have any say in choosing her husband. In 1946 she was married to Johnniebo. He was tall, good-natured and loved to tease Kenojuak. At first she did not want to have anything to do with Johnniebo. Soon she became fond of him. Their marriage was happy. It was a close and loving one. They had several children. Some died as babies or when very young.

Johnniebo and Kenojuak

TO QUEBEC FOR TREATMENT

All Inuit had to go every year to Cape Dorset. There they were X-rayed. They had physical and dental examinations. Those with tuberculosis were taken south to hospitals. Tuberculosis, or T.B., is a disease of the lungs.

Kenojuak had T.B. and had to go south for treatment. She refused to go until she had seen Johnniebo. He was away on a hunting trip. In the meantime Kenojuak had a baby son. Because she had to go to the hospital, she gave her baby to cousins. They adopted him.

On her way to Cape Dorset Kenojuak met Johnniebo. She would not see him again for three and a half years.

IN HOSPITAL

After a long journey, mainly by ship, Kenojuak arrived at the hospital. It was in Quebec City. The Inuit already there were pleased to see her. Now they could hear news of their families.

In late 1953, Kenojuak had been in hospital for almost two years. She received the bad news that both her children had died. They had eaten bad walrus meat. Johnniebo had also been very ill but had recovered.

HER FIRST HANDICRAFT WORK.

When she was well enough to be out of bed, Kenojuak began to do handicrafts. She did beadwork, sewing, and leather work. The work done by Kenojuak and other Inuit was sold. This gave them some money, which was helpful to them.

HOME AGAIN

In May 1955 Kenojuak was on her way home by ship. When she saw the ice floes in the Arctic waters she was filled with great joy. She was happy even though she was seasick. It was wonderful to see the Baffin coastline. It was so familiar to her.

What joy, too, to be with her husband again! Johnniebo was in Cape Dorset. He was helping to unload the annual supply ship. When he had finished his work, they travelled to their home.

LEARNING OLD SKILLS AGAIN
AND NEW ONES

Food was scarce that fall. To earn money, the Inuit made carvings. Their work was sold mainly through the Hudson's Bay Company.

Now Kenojuak had to learn many skills again. The other women had to show her how to sew with caribou thread. Kenojuak began making designs from sealskin. She sold them.

Kenojuak showed she had skill in art forms. She was given paper and pencils. She was asked to draw whatever was in her mind. When she showed her drawings, she was happy with the good comments she received. Kenojuak was also happy with the value given to her work.

Her role as a mother and as an Inuit woman always came first with Kenojuak.

A GREAT EVENT

A great event took place in 1959. The Inuit of Cape Dorset formed the West Baffin Eskimo Co-operative. Some of the drawings done by Inuit were made into prints. People in southern Canada saw them for the first time in Stratford, Ontario. They thought the prints were exciting. One of Kenojuak's first designs was in that exhibit.

STARS IN A FILM

The National Film Board of Canada decided to make a film of Cape Dorset. The film was to show the traditional way of life among the Inuit. Most exciting of all, it was to star Kenojuak and Johnniebo.

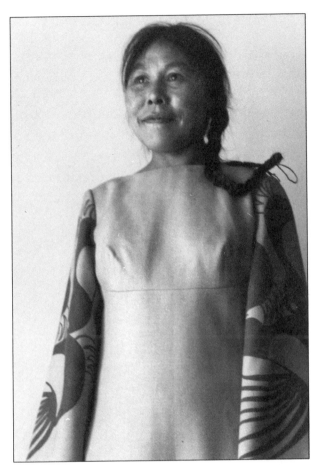

Kenojuak in garment showing textile printing.

FAMILY AND COMMUNITY LIFE

Soon Kenojuak and Johnniebo had enough money to buy a canoe. This meant Johnniebo was able to hunt alone. He did not have to go with other hunters in their canoes. Often their sons went with their father.

Kenojuak and Johnniebo adopted a baby daughter. Then they had their own daughter. The parents were very fond of both their daughters.

HOW THE INUIT EARNED
THEIR LIVING

The Inuit had always depended on the land and sea for their living. Trading companies wanted them to trap fox to sell. When the fur trade dried up, the Inuit became very poor. Then they returned to the land and the sea for their food. Carving became another way for them to earn money. Johnniebo continued to hunt to provide food for his family.

Kenojuak engraving on a metal plate.

KENOJUAK AS AN ARTIST

Kenojuak was singled out as an important Inuit artist. She received widespread recognition and a number of honours.

In 1967 Kenojuak was given the Order of Canada. This was in honour of her ability as an artist. Johnniebo went with Kenojuak to Ottawa where she received the Order. This was Kenojuak's first trip south since her stay in the hospital. This time she and Johnniebo went in an airplane.

In May 1969 Kenojuak and Johnniebo went to Ottawa again. They had been asked to share in the work of a carved wall drawing. This was to be shown in the Canadian pavilion at the World's Fair. The 1970 World's Fair was held in Osaka, Japan. Kenojuak and Johnniebo were to be in Ottawa for three months. So they took their children with them.

When they went back to Cape Dorset they were able to buy a new canoe and a motor.

CHANGE

For the winter, most of the Inuit gave up their camps on the coasts. In the summer they sometimes went back to their camps. At this time, the Inuit also decided to live in places like Cape Dorset. There they had many benefits. They had housing suited to the long cold winters. Their children could go to school. Medical care was on hand when parents or children became ill.

MORE CHANGE

At one time the Inuit used sleds to travel over the sea ice and over land. The sleds were pulled by a team of dogs. Now they can speed along on a Ski-Doo. You can read the story of how the Ski-Doo was invented. This is in the story of Armand Bombardier in this book.

It is interesting to know that until recently the Inuit did not have last names. They had been given numbers. Most chose their fathers' names. Johnniebo did this. His father's name was "Ashevak". Kenojuak, however, still signs her work as she always has, "Kenojuak".

ANOTHER HONOUR AND TRAVEL

Another honour came to Kenojuak. One of her designs was used on a Canadian stamp in 1970. One was used again in 1993.

Twice Kenojuak went to Halifax. She loved that city, partly because it was close to the sea. The first time Johnniebo went with her. The second time Kenojuak took an exhibit of sculpture, drawings, and prints. These were the work of both Kenojuak and Johnniebo.

Kenojuak travelled to Rotterdam. She attended the opening of an exhibition of her work. Her work has been in many group exhibitions. It has also been featured in several shows.

By 1985 she had made more than 1,800 drawings.

The 86¢ stamp with Kenojuak's drawing "The Owl".

JOHNNIEBO'S DEATH

In September 1972 Johnniebo had severe pains in his stomach. He was taken to the nursing station. The fog was thick and heavy. Airplanes could not land in Cape Dorset. Only surgery could save Johnniebo's life. No doctor could get there to do the operation. So Johnniebo died. He is buried in a gravesite behind the house in which Kenojuak lives. He was mourned by Kenojuak and their family. He was greatly loved by them.

MARRIAGE AND HOME

Kenojuak married again but only for a short time. Her second husband died in 1977. Today she lives with her third husband and her six children.

Beside Kenojuak's house is a small canvas tent. In bad weather Kenojuak uses this as her place to carve. In good weather she works out-of-doors. She continues to draw. Her hope is that her works of art will provide for her children.

HER WORK

One of her favourite subjects has been the owl. No two drawings are exactly the same. Some of the other subjects of her drawings have been camp scenes, sea goddesses, various animals and people.

She has not used traditional myths and legends very much. She explains that she did hear such stories as a child. Now she does not remember them. So she does not want to make drawings about them.

Kenojuak has said, "When I am dead, I am sure there will still be people discussing my art."

Kenojuak is famous throughout the world. With her art she has brought fame and honour not only to Canada, but especially to the Inuit people.

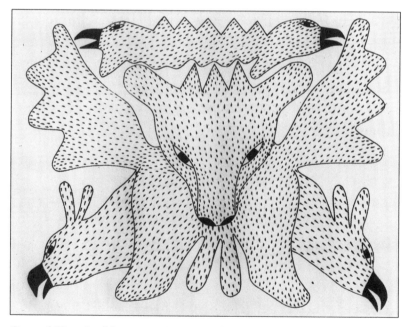

One of Kenojuak's engravings entitled *Composition*.

Another of Kenojuak's works called *Arctic Gulls*.

Antonine Maillet

by

Joan Maass

A VOICE FOR ACADIA

"I knew that if I were to be a writer, I would have to be an *Acadian* writer." Antonine Maillet remembers feeling this way when she was still a child. She knew even then exactly what she wanted to be. And Acadia's tragic history helped to inspire her writing. Maillet is very proud of her Acadian roots. This pride is shown in her famous stories and plays.

The history that means so much to Maillet began about 400 years ago. At that time the first settlers of Acadia came from France. The region they called "Acadia" is now part of our Maritime Provinces.

BRITAIN AND FRANCE AT WAR

The French settlers were followed by British colonists. France and Britain began to fight over their colonies in North America. In 1713 Acadia became a British colony. But Britain and France still did not make peace. Each wanted to own all the land that had been settled in North America at that time.

A PEACEFUL PEOPLE

The French-speaking Acadians wanted to keep their own language and culture. They refused to take sides with either Britain or France. The Acadians were a peaceful people. They worked hard and made a good living. They built dikes and rescued land from the sea. This land was very fertile. They became fishermen and fur traders too. They wished to be an independent people. But a cruel fate awaited them.

EXILE

By 1755 the battles between Britain and France for control of North America had increased in fury. The British feared that the Acadians might side with France. The British also wanted the fertile farmlands of the Acadians. So they chose to do a terrible thing. They sent the Acadians into exile. Some ten thousand men, women, and children were put into ships and sent away. They were sent south to other British colonies. Husbands were separated from their wives and parents from their children. The Acadians faced a hard life far from home. But there's more to their story.

Exile of the Acadians

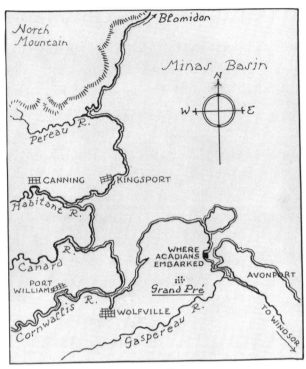
Map showing part of Acadia.

RETURN TO A HOMELAND

In 1763 Britain and France finally signed a peace treaty. This treaty gave Britain all the French colonies in North America. The exiled Acadians were then allowed to return to their homeland. Over 300 families walked all the way back from Boston to the area now called Digby County. Digby County is in Nova Scotia. These families found that their best lands had been taken over by the British. But they started once more to make homes for themselves. Today there are 300,000 descendants of the orginal Acadians who suffered so much.

Maillet makes the Acadia of the past real to us today. Her characters also speak to us of present-day life in Acadian communities.

ANTONINE MAILLET'S CHILDHOOD

Antonine Maillet was born in 1929 in the village of Bouctouche, New Brunswick. She grew up there. She was the fourth girl and the eighth of nine children. Her parents, Leonide and Virginie, had been school teachers. They both read a lot. At the age of three, Antonine heard her first story: "The Three Bears." From that moment on she fell in love with storytelling. She made up her own stories and told them to her family. Then she decided to write down her stories. As a child she wrote little skits for her family to take part in. "I never describe a city or large town in my books, because my childhood was in the woods, in the fields, by the sea," she says.

Maillet (on left) and childhood friend.

THE FIRST MAILLETS

There is a family legend that the Maillets were first known in 1603 in Paris. At that time there were three brothers who were master masons. The mallet was their main tool for building churches. That's how Antonine got her family name. "Maillet" means "mallet".

A PRIZEWINNER

As a college student in New Brunswick Maillet began to write plays. She won first prize in Canada's Dominion Drama Festival. After college she went on to receive a degree from the University of Montreal. She also received a degree from Laval University in Quebec City. She became a teacher. She also did research for Radio-Canada in Paris.

Graduation

INTEREST IN LANGUAGE

Maillet has a great interest in language. She has shown how the French language has changed over the centuries. The characters in her novels and plays speak a language that is clearly Acadian. Her Acadian is a blend of the French spoken today and the French spoken centuries ago. It is spiced with the accent of her own area of New Brunswick.

Maillet in a library — 1977.

A FIRST NOVEL... AND MORE

Antonine Maillet's first novel was written in 1958. Since then she has published 25 novels, plays, and children's stories. In many of her tales the main character is a strong woman. This woman tries to express the soul of her people. Maillet writes of the hardships her ancestors suffered during their long trip back to Acadia. Her stories also tell of the Acadians' struggle to win back the land from the sea. Her work is full of human disagreements too. Little guys battle "big shots". Nasty gossips are crushed. Her tales contain the special humour and down-to-earth wisdom of Acadians.

LA SAGOUINE

The play *La Sagouine* was Maillet's first big hit. ("La sagouine" means "the slattern" or "the slut" in English.) La Sagouine herself is a 72-year-old cleaning woman. She tells her story as she scrubs the floor. She's a former prostitute who is now the wife of Gapi, an Acadian fisherman. She's a very strong woman with a sly sense of humour. She has opinions on everything. Here she is greeting her audience:

"Maybe I got a dirty face 'n cracked skin but, Mister, my hands are white! My hands are white 'cause I had 'em in water all my life. Spent my life cleaning. It don't mean I ain't in rags. I been cleanin' for others.... They give us their ol' stuff 'n their ol' clothes....When you've seen a velvet hat on a lady's head fer ten years, first you kind of like it, 'n you wanna have it. Then it starts gettin' bumpy 'n ends up lookin' like a buckwheat pancake. That's when they give it to you."

And here is La Sagouine talking about the Second World War:

"Lucky thing they was the war! What would we have done, all of us, without it? Ah! Times had become pretty rough. We could of very well croaked like stray animals in their holes. But they was the war just in the nick of time to save us fr'm poverty. Cause in 'em days, seems even the rich folks had a tough time makin' ends meet. So us—well, us we couldn' even make one end meet. Lucky thing they was the war.... In 'em days the army gave good wages, 'n even sent cheques to the women that had their men at war.... That was twenty years ago...."

La Sagouine was a huge success. Actress Viola Léger first played the part in Montreal in 1972. Both critics and audiences loved the play. It was popular throughout Canada, and it also played in Paris. It went on to become a television series.

A SURPRISE

There is a story that Viola Léger once came to a party at the University of Moncton in New Brunswick. She stayed in a corner and scrubbed the floor. Nobody knew she was acting. They thought she was just there to clean. She suddenly stood up and became La Sagouine. She began to speak loudly in La Sagouine's Acadian dialect. She spoke about the many wrongs she and her people have suffered. The guests were amazed.

La Sagouine, like Maillet herself, has become a powerful spokesperson for her people. She is a symbol of the harsh realities of everyday life.

Viola Léger as La Sagouine.

HONOURS FOR "LA SAGOUINE"

A theme park called "Le Pays de la Sagouine" (La Sagouine's Country) was opened at Bouctouche in 1992. This honours Maillet's famous heroine. The park attracts many visitors who learn about Acadia's history and culture. "La Sagouine has now her homeland," says Maillet.

A PRIZE FOR PELAGIE

In 1979 *Pélagie-la-Charette* was published. In English it is *Pélagie: The Return to the Homeland*. The story of *Pélagie* takes place in the 1770s. With her cart and oxen, this exiled heroine struggles to return to Acadia. *Pélagie* is rated a masterpiece. It won for Antonine Maillet the "Prix Goncourt" from France. This was a very high honour for Maillet. She was the first writer in North America to win this prize. It is one of many prizes and honours she has earned over the years.

TWO SPECIAL HOMES

Antonine Maillet spends her summers writing at the lighthouse she owns at Bouctouche. She also has a home on Antonine Maillet Avenue in Montreal. How wonderful it must be to live on a street named after you!

Maillet celebrating the publication of her children's books.

Biographies

Bernice Cleator (Mrs. K. J.) is a retired classroom teacher and is now a literacy tutor. She is Past Secretary of the North Bay and Area Literacy Council. Bernice is a writer of other material, mostly travel articles which have been published.

M. J. Collins (Mike) has been a Laubach volunteer for many years. He is an ex-farmer, retired civil servant, and a WWII veteran. He has had short stories and articles published in North America.

Freda Hudson emigrated from England at the age of six. She has five children and seven grandchildren. She is past chairperson of the Townshipper Reading Council, a past Director of Laubach Literacy of Canada, and is also an active tutor.

Andrea Jeffery has been a tutor with READ Saint John for seven years. She is currently tutoring, is the Treasurer, and is on the training team. Andrea is one of the Laubach Literacy New Brunswick Writers and involved in getting their stories published and distributed. She enjoys reading, writing, and creating word puzzles for her students and her children.

Joan Maass has a B.A. in Library Studies from Concordia University, Montreal. From 1977 to 1990 she was employed at the McLennan Library, McGill University. She has been involved in literacy work for several years and since 1987 has been editor of *Literacy Connections*, issued by Laubach Literacy of Canada. She is also a member of the Publications Committee of L.L.C. Joan is married and has two grown children and one grandchild.

Gladys E. Neale has been in educational publishing for most of her career, mainly with Macmillan of Canada. There she became Director and eventually Senior Vice President. She has been active in the field of literacy since 1972. She is now a Director of Laubach Literacy of Canada and Chairman of the Publications Committee.

Jan Sanderson has nine years of writing experience. She has been a Laubach tutor for almost two years and is currently the editor of the Laubach Literacy's York-Simcoe branch newsletter.

Resource Books

Melville, Douglas A.; *Canadians and the Victoria Cross*, Vanwell Publishing, Ltd., St. Catherines, Ont. 1987.

Smith, Sir Arthur; *The Victoria Cross*, Barker Ltd., London, England. 1977.

The Canadian Encyclopedia; Mynarski, Andrew Charles, Publisher Hurtig M., Edmonton, 1988, Book 3.

Mortimer, Hilda; *You Call me Chief: Impressions of the Life of Dan George*, Doubleday Canada Ltd., Toronto. 1982.

Bruce, Harry; *Maud, The Life of L.M.Montgomery*, Bantam Seal, Toronto. 1992.

Laurence, Margaret; *Dance on the Earth*, McClelland and Stewart, Toronto. 1989.

Stanley, Della M.M.; *Louis Robichaud, A Decade of Power*, Nimbus Publishing Ltd., Halifax, N.S. 1984.

Carr, Emily; *Growing Pains,* Oxford University Press, Toronto. 1946.

Shadbolt, Doris; *Emily Carr*. Douglas and McIntyre, Vancouver/Toronto. 1979.

Tippett, Maria; *Emily Carr, A Biography,* Oxford University Press, Toronto. 1979.

Webb, Michael; *Armand Bombardier, Inventor of the Snowmobile*, Copp Clark Pitman, Mississauga, Ont. 1991.

Precious, Carol; *J.-Armand Bombardier*, (The Canadians), Fitzhenry & Whiteside, Markham, Ont. 1984.

Blodgett, Jean; *Kenojuak*, Firefly Books, Willowdale,. Ont. 1985.

Lévesque René; *Memoirs*, McClelland and Stewart, Toronto. 1956.

Maillet, Antonine; *La Sagouine*, translated by Luis de Céspedes, Simon and Pierre, Toronto. 1979.

Maillet, Antonine; *Pélagie, The Return to a Homeland*, translated by Philip Stratford, Doubleday, New York and Toronto. 1982.